I Heard a Voice

To dear Millie
With love in Jesus

Jo D. Brennan

I Heard a Voice

by Jo D Brennan

Copies may be obtained from the following addresses:-

CMS Bookstore
93 Bathurst St, Sydney NSW 2000 Australia
Ph: +61 2 9284 6700
Fx: +61 2 9284 6742
Email: cms@citychristianbooks.com.au
Web: www.citychristianbooks.com.au

St Barnabas Church, Broadway
PO Box 64, Broadway NSW 2007
Ph: (02) 9211 3496
Fax: (02) 9211 6885
Email: office@barneys.org.au

ISBN 0-9588455-5-7

Cover design by Graham Wade
Text typeset by Bruce Welch
Set in Garamond Book 11.5 point

Printed in Australia by Southwood Press
76-82 Chapel Street, Marrickville 2204

Dedicated to

my sister

Marjie

who always looked

after me as aur

mother asked her

to do.

Introduction

I had three reactions to my reading of Jo Brennan's *"I Heard A Voice"*. The first was of pleasure, at the enjoyable and readable style of her prose. It is easy to understand why, when occasion either gave opportunity or required her to write, what she produced was appreciated and used by others.

My next reaction was to admire her courage. She has been prepared to bare her soul and to allow others to know something of her own spiritual pilgrimage, her doubts, her fears, and her failures, as well as her deep desire to follow Jesus in obedience and sincere discipleship.

My third reaction was personal. It has been my calling in life to occupy pulpits and platforms and to be involved in a public ministry of encouraging others to believe in Jesus and to follow him. If one spends time with those to whom one preaches it is not long before you are humbled by learning of the life experiences of those whom you presume to teach. The 'soul-making' actions of God with his children, their obedience and faith, their stumbles and recoveries, their sufferings and joys, their pains ... often self inflicted ... their cross bearing, their courage and loyalty, leave one with a sense of reverent awe. Any preacher who reads Jo's account will be reminded of this.

If the Psalmist can say that the death of his saints is "precious" to God (Psalm 116:15), we can say that their life is a matter of deep concern to Him too, and that he watches over them with loving purpose. We must be grateful to Jo for her willingness to allow us to view her in her relationship with the Lord whom she serves.

Harry Goodhew
Figtree NSW
November 2002

A chance meeting between Oh and Jo
leads to studying the Bible together with
Oh's friends in modern English, 2002

Acknowledgments

I wish to thank Archbishop Harry Goodhew for his very kind introduction to my book.

I want to thank my sister and her husband, Marjie and Bill Maher, who always lovingly looked after our mother and aunt Marj, freeing me to go overseas, and to acknowledge the loving life-time support of my mother's brother and sisters, the late Keith, Kath and Marj Tulloch, which has enabled me to publish this book.

I also wish to thank CMS, SIM, and Colombo City Mission and all our prayer-partners for their faithful support through the years, without which this story would not have taken place.

I wish to acknowledge for their writing tuition, first Mrs Patricia Chapman when I was her pupil at Stanmore School, then the late Ivy Bailey of U3A and Donna Manser of U3A. I thank Pat Rich and members of The Australian Christian Writer's Fellowship and my writing mentor the Rev David Nicholas for all their kind advice and encouragement, my editor Ruth Colman for her patient, capable editing, Jackie Meyer for her good advice, Jean Crawford and Dorothy Dodds for their typing, and Ruth Crawford for her proof-reading. I am deeply grateful to my computer support teacher Graham Lees for his patient, capable tuition and help, and to Graham Wade for so kindly and skilfully doing my book-cover and photography. Finally I thank Bruce Welch of Southwood Press for all his help.

I acknowledge that without the skilled help, kindness and encouragement of all, this book could not have been published. It's not just my book, it's our book, and I thank God for giving me such friends and helpers. May God bless you for the contribution of your gifts and skills to the producing of this book.

Jo Brennan

November 14th 2002

Preface

I was driving up the road to the Blue Mountains when I asked my companion, Dulcie Levitt, "When did you first believe in God, Dulcie?"

"When I was four years old," she replied.

"That was very young!" I remarked in surprise. "How did it happen?"

"Our mother told my twin sister and me that if we needed help when she wasn't around we should ask God, and he would send an angel to help us," Dulcie said. "We'd been given new button-up shoes, and my button came undone. We both tried to do it up, but the new leather was too stiff for our little fingers. Mum was doing the washing, and she'd told us not to go near her when she was boiling the sheets over the fire. My sister said to me, "We can't ask Mummy. Let's ask God to send an angel to do it up.""

I said, "All right. Let's keep our eyes open when we ask, so we can see the angel." We stood together in the back-yard and asked God to send an angel, but nothing happened. I was so disappointed that I began to wonder whether God and angels were really true. Although I shouldn't have, I went to Mum and told her what had happened. "Mummy, why didn't God send an angel?" I asked.

"I suppose because he knows I'm here to do it for you," she replied. "Now you go and play, and when I've finished the boiling I'll come and do it up for you." So we walked back down the yard. When we got there I said, "I think I'll have another go at doing up that button." I knelt down to try again, and stared at my shoe. The button was already done up! My twin and I went back to the exact spot in the yard where we'd stood to ask God and we thanked him for sending the angel."

"What a wonderful story, Dulcie! Thank you for sharing it with me. Did you have any more experiences of God after that? "

"Oh, yes," she replied, "After that God often spoke to us."

"What did he say?" I asked curiously, reminding myself to keep my eye on the road, and thinking, Who would ever have guessed that this little grey-haired woman in her old overcoat and pink hat would have had such wonderful experiences of God!

"We didn't try to remember," Dulcie replied. "We thought that everyone heard God speaking to them. But one time I remember was when we were playing outside in the winter-time, and God said, 'Go inside, now, children.' We went inside, and after that the snow came down."

"And did you continue to hear God speaking to you after you grew up?" I asked.

"Not in the same way," she replied, "but God spoke to me in other ways."

Dulcie went on to tell of her interest in plants, and how she had worked in the Land Army during the second world war. After the war ended she took more training in that field, then went with CMS *(Church Missionary Society)* to the Northern Territory and spent twenty-five years working amongst Aboriginal people. A book she'd written had just been published, giving the botanical names as well as the Aboriginal names and uses for many of the plants of Arnhem Land, and with valuable papers of hers are stored in the archives of the Aboriginal institute, AIATSIS, in Canberra. A book of her work has been published and is available in the twenty-first century under the title *Tribal Customs.*

How does God usually communicate with people? Perhaps not always in such spectacular ways as he did with these two faith-filled children, but I've found that God drops clues, and if we follow the clues there will be more. Come with me, then, as I retrace the clues God dropped into my life, and tell you what happened when I followed them.

Chapter 1

As a child I had no idea what an important part Pokolbin, the place of my mother's family home, would play in my teens, when I faced the first big cross-roads in my life.

We loved "Glen Elgin", the old weatherboard home at Pokolbin where our mother grew up. The old house had many voices. Its timbers creaked when strong westerly winds blew across the Hunter Valley, and audibly cracked as they cooled down at the end of a scorching summer's day. In winter, the lounge-room fire whispered softly in the grate and roared up the chimney when extra wood and coal were put on. On cold nights we sat around it with our uncle and aunts, Keith, Kath and Marj, the unmarried members of the Tulloch family, all quietly reading our library books by the light of the softly hissing pressure lamp in the days before TV. We loved the sounds of the night after we went to bed, the steady croaking of frogs down in the dam, the occasional clack of the windmill sails. These made cherished memories, but my favourite time of the day was the late afternoon when my sister Marjie called to me, "Jo, let's go up to the gates!"

We followed the car tracks through rows of grape vines to the main road, where two tall concrete pillars supported iron gates, marking the entrance to Tulloch's vineyards. Climbing up we sat one on each pillar, looking out across the yellow grassed western plain.

Far down on the flats, cattle would be slowly moving towards higher ground to spend the night, away from low-lying evening mists. They occasionally bellowed to one another, and we held our noses and bellowed back in such a good imitation that they often answered us. To the north, shadows deepened on the Broken Back Range and the sky changed. Clouds flushed with reflected light and colour from the setting sun, and we watched, entranced, until the colour faded and the evening star appeared. Then we climbed down and went home.

At eighteen my sister commenced her nursing training at Cessnock District Hospital, seven miles from Pokolbin, and in Sydney, at sixteen I was granted a part scholarship to study art at the East Sydney Technical College, which we referred to as "tech." On the last day of the second year of my course the teacher paused beside the painting I was doing and remarked, "Your colours are too pretty!" She chose two other students' paintings, both executed in strong, dark colours, to pin up before the class and commend.

"This one has interesting colour," she observed, "and this one has arresting design." Then our classes were over for the year.

Is this what tech means? I thought as I travelled home on the train. Would I have to change my whole idea of beauty and try to paint to please my teacher? Art would no longer be a joyous means of self expression.

Sitting on the gatepost at Pokolbin a week later, an alarming thought struck me. How would I ever learn to paint a sunset if I couldn't use "pretty" colours? The hour I loved was spoilt, and my heart filled with a sense of poignant loss. I won't even be able to enjoy a sunset if I stay at tech much longer, I thought.

"You don't have to stay at tech you know. Tech is not the same as school. You can leave if you want to."

It was as though someone had spoken. Not aloud, but to my thoughts. Discouragement vanished, and excitement took its place. *I didn't have to stay at tech! I could leave if I wanted to!*

Where the words had come from that would change my life, I didn't know. Suddenly it seemed to be the most sensible thing to do. I didn't want to do "commercial art," I only wanted to paint landscapes and portraits, and I could do that as a hobby, and earn my living some other way. I discussed the idea with my mother and my Aunt Marj, who was a teacher.

"You're eighteen now," my mother said. "You must make up your own mind," and Aunt Marj agreed with her. I didn't return to tech. But now I had to decide what to do instead. "You and your mother can stay here while you think about it," my Aunt Kathleen offered generously. "There's no hurry to decide."

My sister Marjie was soon to marry her fiance Bill, a member of the Australian Air Force, and I occupied my time painting a landscape for their wedding present. At the end of each day I walked up to the gates. One evening as I watched the sunset I thought, Where is God, the maker of all this beauty? Is it possible to find him? To know him? The body language of a stark dead gum tree, its bare branches silhouetted against the sky, seemed to cry out, *"God! Where are you?"* The only answer was the appearance of the evening star.

Each week my sister rode her bicycle out to Pokolbin on her day off, and she told me enthralling stories about hospital life. It occurred to me that perhaps I, too, could become a nurse. "Royal Prince Alfred Hospital's where you ought to train," my uncle's wife, a former RPA theatre-sister, advised me. "You might want to go to England when you finish, and the RPA certificate is recognised overseas."

I applied to RPA and was accepted. At the end of my first day in the wards I threw myself down on my bed and sighed with deep contentment, "I've found what I want to do most in all the world. I just want to be a nurse."

Christmas 1947 in A3, RPA's Orthopaedic Ward (Jo's first ward).

"Give that to Mr Jones," a senior nurse directed me a few months later, thrusting a small kidney dish into my hands. It held a syringe of insulin. I wondered why she didn't come with me, but as we'd practised on a dummy in the preliminary training school I walked obediently up the long ward carrying the precious injection. But when I came to the patient's bed, my legs carried me right past, out the door and back along the verandah. Turning in at the end of the ward, I took a deep breath and started again. This time I managed to stop at the patient's bed.

"Roll up your sleeve please, Mr Jones," I instructed the patient, (a veteran of many injections) Giving the flesh a professional rub with cotton wool, I pinched up the skin, poised the needle, then shut my eyes and jabbed. A squeal of pain split the air. It was my own, for the needle had gone right through the patient's skin and into my own finger!

Mr Jones roared with laughter. "Have another go, Nurse," he offered generously. The second time I got the needle into the right place.

If I was nervous at giving my first injection, it was as nothing compared to the first time I had to work in the operating theatre. "If the surgeon hands an instrument to you when you're not scrubbed up," the sister told us at our orientation lecture, "you should take the instrument at its extreme tip, so that you don't contaminate his sterile glove with your hand."

No surgeon is ever likely to hand *me* an instrument, I thought, very conscious of my junior status. The first time I worked in the theatre, in the middle of an operation the surgeon turned around and held out an instrument to me. As I approached the gowned, masked figure, panic descended on me. "*Take it at the extreme tip*" came floating back to me from the sister's lecture. I took hold of the instrument at its extreme tip— but at the wrong end!

"You touched me!" the surgeon gasped. Quickly recovering himself, he strode out of the theatre, stripping off his contaminated glove as he went. There was a buzz around the operating table. "What happened?"

"She touched him."

"Oh, she touched him!"

"Yes, she touched him. He's gone to change his glove." Mercifully the surgeon returned quickly and the operation resumed as if nothing had happened. The nurse from the next theatre came in to see how we were getting on, and in a hushed whisper I told her the terrible thing that I'd done. When I came to the surgeon's remark, "You touched me," she whispered loudly in my ear, "Why didn't you say, 'Yes, weren't you thrilled?'"

Silent laughter shook me and my fear fled. When fear vanishes, common sense returns. A few weeks later when a surgeon asked me to put on sterile gloves and gown and stand opposite him gently retracting the breathing lung of a child with my hand while he performed a "blue baby" heart operation, there was no hint of nervousness as I eagerly obeyed. Filled with awe, I watched the living heart of the child leaping against my gloved hand while the surgeon operated.

There were times of sadness, too, during the four years' training, such as when Win, a mother of six, died in medical ward, and when a young mother died in the neuro-surgery ward. She had been a concert pianist, and as I removed her wedding ring to be given to the family it seemed to me tragic that one who had played beautiful music would never play again. The worst was that she had a young baby, who now would never know how much his mother had loved him.

My friends went out on dates with medical students, and sometimes they made dates for me, and we moved slowly around the dance-floor to the cry of a trombone. Somehow, I never made a date myself, so consequently it was a surprise to my friends when I was the first of our little group to become engaged. It was to the son of a cattle-station manager in Queensland where I spent my first-year holidays. On my second-year holidays he came down to Sydney, but by the time my third-year holidays arrived I realised I was not really in love, and I broke the engagement.

My most realistic moments came when I was alone, thinking deeply about the meaning of life. Standing at an upstairs window of the nurses' home looking across the city, the glory of the sunset brought to my mind the same questions as I'd experienced at Pokolbin. Where was God? How could we find him? Was it possible to really know him?

Jo when training to be a nurse at RPA in 1950

In a second-hand bookshop I discovered a book on the historical life of Jesus. Eagerly I bought it and took it back to the hospital. It was full of theological jargon that I didn't understand, but I persevered, hoping that at last I was about to find God. Instead, I came to the part where the author expressed his opinion that Jesus had hoped to establish an earthly kingdom, and when he realised he had lost, he "flung himself upon the wheel of fate and ended up on a cross."

Putting the book down in deep disappointment, I did not read any more. Didn't even I, with no theological training whatsoever, know just from listening to sermons that Jesus had prophesied his own death long before it happened? How could he be planning an earthly kingdom when he had clearly said to Pilate, the Roman governor, *"My kingdom is not of this world" John 18:36 RSV*

As children, our mother had encouraged us to write poetry. I had not done so since then, but now I tried to express my thoughts and longings in verse:

Witness the stunted souls along the way
Who ceased to wonder,
Thinking to compromise,
By stunted acts of conscience, to appease
The power that seemed too complex to perceive.

I didn't want to be a stunted soul, trying to appease a God I didn't know. I wanted to find the Great Artist who had created the universe, and communicate with him.

On Graduation Day we excitedly pinned stiffly starched veils on our heads and blossomed into Junior Sisters. My four years of general training were finished.

But I still had not found God.

Chapter 2

"CRUELTY TO PATIENTS IN MENTAL HOSPITALS"

The newspaper reports disturbed me. Could it be true? My mother and I had moved, to share house with my sister and her husband in a suburb where a mental institution was situated. Looking over the wall from the window of a bus, it looked so peaceful inside. Neatly mown lawns and shady trees gave an impression of stately beauty that belied the media reports. What really was the truth, I wondered? As the bus continued to pass by, an idea began forming in my mind. There was a six months waiting list at the hospital to which I'd applied to do midwifery training. Perhaps I could get a job in the mental hospital while I waited, and then I'd see whether these media reports were true or not. Pulling the bus-cord, I alighted and walked through the entrance gates, then followed an arrow pointing to the matron's office. A stately looking woman in white invited me in, and I explained my need of a few months' work.

"We don't take people on that basis," she said. "You would have to do your psychiatric training, and since you've completed your general, that would take you two years instead of three. But anyway," – she looked me over speculatively – I don't think you could do it. You don't look very strong to me!"

Not very strong! From childhood when anyone implied that I was not very strong – an impression given by my thin arms and legs and my glasses – my immediate reaction was always to prove them wrong.

"I'd like to try please," I said politely but firmly.

With a sigh of resignation the Matron brought out a set of application papers and pushed them tiredly across the desk. "Fill those in and return them to me " she said shortly. "And don't forget, once you sign those papers you'll have to give a month's notice if you want to leave!"

Putting them triumphantly into my handbag I thanked her and left, but as I walked through the gates the realisation of what I had done hit me. I'd come in merely to inquire, and now, thanks to my impetuous nature, instead of doing obstetrics I'd be spending the next two years behind these long stone walls! Obstetrics would have to wait.

But obstetrics did not wait. A few weeks later I came on duty at 6am and read the night-report, then went straight to the room of our only pregnant patient. Encased in a straitjacket, Jenny lay facing the window of her strong-room, her ankles and arms securely strapped to the sides of the bed. The canvas jacket had worked up, exposing her large white abdomen. I put my hand upon it, and it felt hard. Her wide blue eyes questioned me. "Oo-er! My belly's sore!" she said in a little-girl voice.

Jenny was eighteen, but the psychiatrist had assessed her mental age as eight. Since the onset of pregnancy she had become acutely suicidal and had been kept under full restraint to protect her and her unborn child. Tendrils of fair curly hair, wet with sweat, clung to her temples, and perspiration beaded her forehead and upper lip. I had a look to see what was happening, and was startled to see something dark coming. Never having seen a baby born before, I was almost as naive as Jenny. Could it be the uterus prolapsing?

I was not left long in doubt. As I gazed, the dark object became the baby's head, and it emerged, turned sideways, and was followed by the shoulders. Putting out my hands, I caught it as it was forcefully expelled, wet and slippery. Supporting the head and shoulders with my right hand, I grasped the ankles with my left and raised the feet as the illustration in my sister's midwifery book had shown, to allow any fluid in the mouth to drain out.

The baby was navy blue. As I watched, the small chest was indrawn with an involuntary gasp, and a miraculous tide of pink flowed through the body beginning at the head and sweeping to the feet, and I found myself holding a bright pink, vigorously crying infant. At that moment the charge nurse walked in with the doctor, whom she had gone to call. I laid the baby on the bed and stepped back for the doctor to deliver the placenta.

After he had gone, pandemonium broke loose. The nurses came in, followed by the working patients (those with jobs) all wanting to see the new baby whose crying had announced his arrival to the whole ward.

"Oh, isn't he beautiful!" "Look at his little hands!" "What tiny feet he has."

"I want to see my baby! Let me see him!" Jenny was struggling to sit up, still restrained by her straitjacket. Her plea and the joy of the working patients who stood around the bed, buckets and brooms in their hands, imprinted the moment on my memory. Charge Nurse Steer loosened the ties of the canvas jacket so that Jenny could lift her head and look at her baby, and then asked, "Who has bathed a new-born baby before?"

"I have, plenty of times!" I exaggerated. Not as new as this one, I admitted to myself, but I'd bathed small babies in the children's ward during my general training. Having delivered him, I wasn't going to let anybody else bath him! By the time the baby was dressed in the beautiful baby clothes that were ready waiting for him, the charge-nurse had removed Jenny's restraint and bathed her, dressing her in a fresh, pretty night-dress. She stood by to safeguard mother and child while Jenny sat on the side of her bed and nursed her son. Gazing in awe at him, she traced the tiny features softly with her finger, stroking the silken hair, allowing the tiny fingers to curl round one of her own, and gently touching the tiny bootee-clad feet. Then he was taken away from her.

Restraint proved to be no longer necessary for Jenny once her baby was born. With nothing left to fear, all her suicidal tendencies vanished, and within a few months she was discharged and re-united with her child.

"I saw Jenny and the baby in the supermarket yesterday," Nurse Steer remarked to me soon after her discharge. "The baby looked so happy and well cared for. Jenny's mother was with her. She's helping her to look after him." Her face glowed with pleasure as she spoke.

Jenny's case seemed to have a happy ending. At least she went home. It was the patients who never went home that concerned me, and the general atmosphere of the place. Many patients had a history of violence, and were restrained, for there were not enough staff. The miracle drugs that would revolutionise psychiatric treatment had not yet been discovered. There seemed to be no hope for the hundreds of patients who filled the state's mental institutions.

The asphalt yard was enclosed by a high wire fence. Patients sat immersed in their own delusions. It all was a far cry from the green lawns and shady trees I had seen from the bus. The seeming hopelessness of it all made me want to get away. Each day after lunch I sat outside the dining-room smoking a cigarette, trying to resist the urge to go to the office to resign. I didn't want to desert the patients and the faithful band of nurses who looked after them, but the urge to throw down my keys and walk out grew stronger by the day.

At last I could resist no longer. Stubbing out my cigarette, I walked down the path to the matron's office. She was not in but a senior sister sat behind her desk.

"I'm sorry Sister," I said. "I've come to resign."

"But Nurse, you've only been here a few months! " she protested. "Couldn't you think about it a little longer?"

"I've been thinking about it for a long time." I replied. "I've tried to stay, but it's no use. I just can't. I've made up my mind to go."

"Well, at least you must give a month's notice." she reasoned. "You agreed to that when you came."

Her words came as a shock. I'd forgotten my contract. My hopes of leaving that day faded.

"All right, I'll write out my resignation tonight," I agreed. At least it was only one more month, and I was relieved that the decision was made.

That evening I sat down at the sun-room table with the writing-pad and sat nibbling the end of a pen. How will I word it? I wondered. What will I say?

"You thought you were serving God by staying in that hospital and looking after those patients, didn't you?" The words jumped unbidden into my mind.

Yes, I suppose that's just what I did think! I admitted in surprise.

"If that's the case, don't you think you had better ask God now, before you leave?"

Yes, I suppose I'd better! I agreed, again in surprise, for it had never occurred to me in my entire life to ask God a question and expect an answer. Putting down the pen, I went into my mother's bedroom for privacy and shut the door, then knelt down beside the bed.

Suddenly the Presence of God was with me in the room, immersing me, body, mind and spirit, in joy so amazing that tears ran down my cheeks, as I silently worshipped. Then, as suddenly as the experience had come, it, had gone again.

I got up from my knees and went out and silently put away the pen and writing pad. Before that experience, nothing could have kept me at the mental hospital. After that, nothing could have driven me away. I interpreted it to mean that God wanted me to stay and help to look after those people for the full two years of my training. He must love them and be pleased with those who were faithfully caring for them.

I had always believed in God and in his Son Jesus Christ, but now I not only believed, I knew that it was true, for I had experienced for myself the reality of God's wonderful presence. I could never be afraid to die now, I thought, for to be in God's presence is more beautiful than anything in this world. I told no one about my experience, for it was too precious to risk scepticism.

After I'd completed my training and left the hospital, the charge nurse with whom I'd shared the experience of the birth of Jenny's baby saw me in the street. Her eyes were shining and her face glowed with happiness as she exclaimed: "You wouldn't recognise the place now! New drugs have been discovered, and patients who were in there for years have gone home. Others who used to wear straitjackets are walking around, going to craft, and going on bus trips. Patients wear their own clothes now, and that old stone wall has been pulled down!"

God's time had come, and our mental hospitals would

never be the same again.

On the last night of my training, as I cleaned out a cupboard I came across a bottle of anaesthetic ether. Removing the rubber cap, I allowed the familiar smell to drift under my nostrils for a moment. What memories it brought back!

If I ever worked in a country hospital I'd need to get more theatre experience, I thought speculatively. Perhaps now was the time to get it. All my friends were still on the staff of my training hospital where I'd been so happy. If I went back, it would be like turning back the clock!

I put the bottle back in the cupboard, but the odour of ether hung on the air. An impossible dream? But perhaps it could be done. I went home and wrote a letter, and the reply came back almost immediately.

I was accepted on the staff of Royal Prince Alfred Hospital to work in the general operating theatres as a junior sister.

Chapter 3

The surgeon was a stout man with compassionate brown eyes and stubby fingers that could perform miracles. After seven hours of delicate work freeing a tumour mass off the brain he suddenly came to the crucial moment when he lifted out the tumour and deposited it in a metal kidney dish which I held out to him. The cavity immediately welled with blood.

"Hot packs!" he ordered abruptly, his forceps poised to receive them. I looked at him blankly. What did he mean? The cavity was not suitable for a sponge, and "patties" of compressed cotton were too small. After six months in the general theatres, I had just come to take the place of the instrument sister who was leaving. For two weeks we had "doubled up," and now, in the middle of an operation she had left the theatre for a few minutes without telling me the next step of the procedure. I looked at the surgeon inquiringly.

"Didn't Sister tell you?" he exploded. Jumping down from his stool he ran around the table to my instrument trolley and bent down, rapidly sorting through the sterile equipment. He came up with a handful of cotton wool, from which he tore pieces and submerged them in a bowl of sterile Ringer's Solution. Testing the temperature with a thermometer as he ran, he stepped back up on his stool and plopped hot, sodden pieces of cotton wool into the brain cavity. Immediately the bleeding stopped flowing, and he was able to cauterise a few still spurting small arteries.

Before that emergency I had no trace of a headache, but when it was past, my head was pounding. Each morning after that, as the heavy entrance door to the Neurosurgery and Psychiatric Unit thudded shut behind me, my head began to ache. I consumed packets of Aspirin until gradually I grew accustomed to the work and the tension eased.

The surgeon for whom I routinely worked was a tall, quiet man who set out to train me to anticipate his needs.

"Routine, Sister, routine! You remember what I used last time." His slim, gloved hand swayed this way and that, urging me to place in it the instrument he required, but refused to name. I set myself to memorise each instrument of every case, going over each step of the day's surgery when I got home. Soaking in a hot bath gave me a good opportunity to practise.

"Periosteal elevators!" I grabbed the soap.

"Bone retractors!" The washer followed the soap with lightning speed into the water. Gradually I became familiar with each stage of the operations, and could slap the correct instrument into that gloved hand without a moment's pause.

Ben, my fellow instrument assistant, worked for the senior surgeon. I greatly admired the way he never appeared to get ruffled. He always knew what to do when things went wrong. I'd never heard anyone else talk about God the way Ben did, calling him "the Lord," as if he knew him personally. Because he could not afford a house in Sydney, his family lived in a small country town while he lived in a room near the hospital and went home only at weekends. He and his wife were praying for a job for him in Sydney, with a house attached. Eventually he got a job in charge of the theatre of a large state hospital, with a home provided in the hospital's grounds.

Ben talked so much about God that I suspected that he was trying to convert me. I thought I was already a Christian, for I'd dedicated my life to God's service at fifteen, when I was confirmed. But I didn't tell Ben. I thought it would be fun to see how he went about converting me! However, the joke was on me, because Ben had something to share that I knew nothing about.

One day he arrived at work with a large book to lend me. It was a Bible-dictionary, and contained information from A to Z about Christianity. I took it off duty with me, and that night sat down and opened it at random and started to read. I'd opened at the letter L, and it said, Luther, Martin: *Justification by faith alone:*

Luther, a 15th century German priest, had tried by much penance and fasting to rid himself of the guilt of his sins, but he still felt guilty. Finally he went to Rome, and there climbed the steps of the great church of St Peter's, on his knees, repeating many prayers on every step. As he did so he remembered something he had read in the Bible:

"For I am not ashamed of the gospel: it is the power of God for salvation to every one who has faith"........"He who through faith is righteous shall live." Romans 1:16, 17 RSV

Suddenly Luther realised that this meant that God accepted him, blotting out his sins and counting him as righteous because of his faith in Jesus Christ. His trying, by his many prayers and penances, to do for himself what Jesus had already done for him on the cross, showed that he had not believed what Jesus had accomplished on the cross. He must believe it, that he was already saved by Jesus' atonement. He was justified, made righteous by Jesus' sacrifice, through faith in it.

As I read it, I realised that I, too, was justified through faith. I'd had faith in Jesus since my childhood, so this meant that I too was saved, but I'd never realised it before. How wonderful! I felt like shouting. I could go to heaven because of what Jesus had done for me!

In the Communion Services of my church I'd heard the same thing, over and over again many times, but had never understood it. I now took down the Bible that my Aunt Marj had given me as a confirmation gift, but which I'd never tried to read. I opened it at Paul's letter to the Romans, and began to read.

The whole world is guilty before God, I read, because no human being has ever succeeded in keeping God's law, and so God has made a different way to be saved, that is, through faith in his Son.

"For no human being will be justified in his sight by the works of the law .....

Since all have sinned and fall short of the glory of God, they are justified by his grace as a gift, through the redemption that is in Christ Jesus, whom God put forward as an expiation through faith in his blood, to be received through faith.

For we hold that a man is justified by faith, apart from works of law."

Romans 3:19-28 RSV

What difference would this amazing truth make in my life?

I was about to find out.

19

Chapter 4

The seventeen-year-old girl lay as if she were asleep, but in fact she was unconscious, her face undamaged by the accident and her shoulder-length brown hair tied back with a blue ribbon. Lornie had been trying to cross Parramatta Road to get to the University when she'd been hit by a truck. "What chance has she?" I asked the Neuro-surgical Registrar as we stood beside her bed. "We've done all we can," he replied pessimistically, "and her level of unconsciousness is still deepening. That means she's still bleeding deep inside her brain, where we can't reach it. There's no more we can do, so your guess is as good as mine." He gestured hopelessly and walked away to hide his own emotion.

He's saying that there's no hope for her, I concluded. She's too young to die! Something that had happened ten years previously suddenly came back to me. My mother had been suffering from a severe migraine, and I'd remembered that Jesus had laid his hands on people and healed them. Standing beside her bed I'd gently laid my hands on her head, and without telling her what I was doing, silently prayed that Jesus would take the headache away. About fifteen minutes later she called out: "You can make me a cup of tea now, darling. My headache's gone!"

I got a shock. Its true! I thought. Jesus still heals today! But perplexity followed. If Jesus still heals today, why don't ministers preach about it, I wondered? I'd never heard a sermon on the subject. And if Jesus still heals today, we could just pray and everyone would get healed, and no one would ever die! The sequence of my reasoning seemed too astounding to have any answer, and I pushed the whole thing down into my subconscious mind and never thought about it again.

Until now. Now I couldn't help thinking about it. If Jesus could heal my mother's headache, couldn't he stop the bleeding inside Lornie's head?

Two days previously, Ben had given me a magazine with an illustration of Jesus raising Jairus's dead daughter to life, and there was an article on putting our faith into practice. If my faith was real, I thought, I must do for Lornie what I'd done for my mother – lay my hands on her head and pray. But I needed privacy in order to really pray. I imagined the ward sister saying in her sharp manner, "What are you doing here, Sister? Go back to your theatre!" Praying that God would give me courage, I paused at the open doorway on my way off duty. The staff had all gone to tea except one nurse who was busy in another area. The second bed had been removed, and Lornie was alone. It's now or never, I thought. The room was filled with sunset light as I quietly crossed the floor and placed my hands on her head. Lifting up my heart in silent prayer, I asked that the healing power of Jesus Christ would touch Lornie's brain and stop the bleeding.

When I left the room I had not the slightest doubt but that God had answered and healed her. Walking up the driveway, I looked up at the sky. The reflected light of the setting sun which had filled Lornie's room was a flaming sunset right across the sky, and to me it celebrated Lornie's healing. Three days later I heard one of the ward nurses exclaiming, "Have you seen Lornie? She's beginning to wake up!"

I could have told you that three days ago, I thought with secret joy.

Gradually she became fully conscious, and there was no mental impairment.An operation was needed to remove blood clots from the brain.The nurses did not shave off her lovely brown hair until after the anaesthetic had been given, so as not to frighten her. Everyone breathed a sigh of relief when she was wheeled out of the theatre, the operation a success.

Every morning two nurses helped her to walk to the verandah and sit in the sun. My surgeon being away, I had time to sit with her and tell her all that had happened.

"Will I ever be able to walk again by myself?" she asked.

"See those jacaranda trees, Lornie?" I replied, indicating the trees whose top branches were level with second floor verandah where we sat."By the time they're in bloom you'll be home."

When the nurse told me that Lornie was dying of meningitis, I couldn't believe it, but when I saw her I feared it could be true. She lay on her side, thin and wasted, a vomit-bowl tucked under her chin, her eyes dull and lethargic. Infection from her sinuses had been seeping into her brain through a hairline fracture that had been missed in the first x-rays. Intravenous antibiotics were dripping into her vein with the hope that the fracture might spontaneously heal over.

I wanted to pray again the way I had done the first time, but she was now in the observation room, right next to the ward sister's office.There was no privacy, and although I prayed desperately for courage, it didn't come. I'm like someone watching a person gradually slipping over a cliff, and refusing to reach out a hand to pull them back, I thought. "Lord, please forgive me, I prayed."Don't heal Lornie through me, but heal her in spite of me."

Lornie's condition suddenly began to improve. She got better so fast that within two weeks she was transferred to the hospital's rehabilitation unit, and within a short time she was discharged, completely well. Three months later when she returned for her routine check-up with the doctor, she was radiantly happy, full of thanks to the dedicated staff, and full of praise to God. "The Lord healed me!" she told her surgeon.

But for Isabella Bennett, a nursing trainee, it was a different story. Isabella's fair skin, dark hair and blue eyes made her beautiful, but it was her shining faith that gave her face a special quality.

One day a discussion arose about what the nurses hoped to do when they finished their training. "What are you hoping to do when you finish, Isabella?" I asked as she was seeing me off. She stood silently with a far off look in her eyes. Not wanting to intrude on her thoughts, I walked quietly away.

I didn't know that she had been suffering from abdominal pain, and in spite of surgery the cause had not been diagnosed. Some time after our conversation she was taken to the theatre again, and this time the cause of her pain was discovered. She was suffering from an advanced stomach cancer which was inoperable.

Isabella told me that she didn't want "anything special" in the way of prayer. "Just ordinary prayer," she said, "and if it's God's will to heal me I'll be healed, but if it's his will to take me home to be with him, I'll be just as pleased."

As the weeks passed, Isabella's pain increased, and those who loved her hoped that God would take her soon, out of her suffering. Before she died Isabella wrote a poem, which after her death was hung on a wall of the nurses' holiday cottage in the Blue Mountains overlooking the Jamieson Valley.

The curtain for me is now parted;
the glorious light has flowed through.
The dark, sin stained life is now over;
I've started living anew.
The Giver of Life, the Lord Jesus
is the Life, the Truth and the Way.
I don't need a soul but my Saviour,
for now I'm a child of the Day.

Search your hearts and find out the answer:
is the Saviour your Saviour today?
Have you claimed yet his precious salvation?
Have you crowned him your Lord of the Way?
Your own trying and striving won't help you,
on him you will have to depend,
and once you have entered his kingdom
he has promised to keep to the end."

Written by Isabella Bennett, who died aged 21 years in her third year of nursing at Royal Prince Alfred Hospital in Sydney

The words of the Apostle Paul in Romans Chapter 8 enabled me to accept death. The whole world is groaning in pain, he wrote, waiting to be set free from the law of death and decay which have been appointed by God for now. Although our souls are already redeemed, the full redemption of our bodies will not take place until Jesus returns, after which there will be no more sickness, sorrow or pain, and no more death.

But I found healing to be there for some who had great faith, just as Jesus promised. A twelve-year-old boy who had been hit by a taxi lay unconscious for weeks, breathing by the aid of a tracheotomy tube inserted in his neck. "Who is the man who sits beside him every day?" I asked a nursing aide, sure that it couldn't be his father, because of the big smile on his face.

"It's his father," she said. "He's a Christian, and he'd gone away from the Lord. Since his son's accident he's come back, and he's sure God is going to heal his son."

One day the nursing aide came to tell me that the boy's condition was worse. "They think he has septicaemia," she said. "His temperature is raging. He's on IV antibiotics, and he's dangerously ill."

That night she pulled a screen around the boy's bed, and his father, the nursing aide and I laid our hands upon him and in the name of Jesus asked for his healing. By morning the fever had subsided, and over the following weeks he recovered completely. The young man with the shock of corn coloured hair who came for his check-up three months later astounded me. Could this be the same boy who had lain at death's door for so long in our ward?

His father's faith had been rewarded.

Chapter 5

It had been a long day in the theatre. Every instrument had to be boiled and put away. Forgetting to tell the theatre nurse where I was going, I went to the deserted x-ray department to relax over a cigarette. On return I found her distraught. "Sister, where have you been?" she asked. "I've been looking for you everywhere! A boy has stopped breathing, and they're on their way down to do an emergency craniotomy!"

Throwing the instruments into the steriliser, I set up the theatre with record speed, and we were just ready in time as the doors swung open to admit the trolley with the patient on it, accompanied by the emergency team.

"I'll never smoke again!" I determined as I went off duty. But I did. After more fruitless attempts to give it up, I realised that I was addicted.

"Tonight I'm going to speak to you on just one verse from the Bible," said our speaker, Sister Joan Massie, at the Christian meeting in the Nurses' Residence where I lived. She read the verse aloud:

"Simon, I have something to say to you." Luke 7:40 RSV

"Jesus had something to say to Simon." Joan continued. "Has Jesus got something to say to you? Perhaps he's been saying it to you for a long time, and you haven't been listening. Put your name in the place of Simon's, and see what Jesus is saying to you."

I tried it. *"Jo, I have something to say to you."* Immediately I knew what it was. I'd thought the feeling of guilt about smoking was just me, but now I knew it had been Jesus speaking to me. If the Lord Jesus had taken the trouble to speak to me, Jo, about smoking, then I wanted to obey him. Because of what Jesus suffered for me on the cross, I never smoked again, nor did I even want to.

When I tried to share with others the marvellous truth of acceptance with God through faith in Jesus Christ, two of my friends found it as wonderful as I did, but others weren't interested. I grieved over their indifference, for I read in my Bible: *"How shall we escape if we neglect such a great salvation?" Hebrews 2:3 RSV* . Would God really send to hell those who rejected his Son, I wondered? The words of a hymn which we sang at church helped me to see that the sorrow I was feeling for the first time for those who are lost was really Jesus' sorrow which he was putting into my heart.

As I longed for people to listen and believe and be saved from hell, I remembered that as a child I'd wanted to be a missionary when I grew up. I began to recall things in my childhood which might possibly mean that God had been preparing me for this purpose.

My father Frank was much older than my mother Dorothy. Tall, white haired with a white moustache and a great sense of humour, he was fifty eight and she twenty eight when they fell in love and married. When their first child, Marjorie, was born, they were deeply happy, but when my mother became pregnant with me she was worried. My father's sight was failing due to glaucoma, and there was a depression looming.

*Dorothy and Frank on their
wedding day, September
1924 at Pokolbin*

"We didn't plan to have another baby, darling," my father said to her on the day I was born, "but God planned it. I may not be here to see it, but you mark my words, you will see. God must have a purpose for this child's life, or he would never have given her to us at such a time."

The time was 1928, and the depression began in 1929. Despite our parents' financial worries, we were happy. Although our father's hair, eyebrows and moustache were white, we never thought of him as old. He was the one who played with us and teased us. We went for walks with our parents along mountain tracks where towering gum trees and green ferns grew and a stream rushed over the rocks. I gathered velvety green moss to take home to make a tiny garden, and we carried home tadpoles in a jam-jar. Once a year our mother took us by steam train to Cessnock, where our uncles drove us out to Pokolbin. Our father always stayed at home to mind the house and tenants.

Jo at one year at Leura NSW,
1929

Mother, father and daughters
Marjie 5 yrs, Jo 2 yrs, 1930

It was at Pokolbin one day that our mother drew us close to her and told us, "Daddy has gone to be with Jesus."

We stayed on at Leura until winter, when one morning our mother found a man's footprints in the snow around our house. Alarmed, she decided to move to Sydney to be near her sister, our Aunt Marj. The sound of wind in the gumtrees was replaced by the metallic clatter of the paperboy's billy-cart going down North Street, Marrickville. Aunty Marj came to live with us and brought two other teachers, who were joined by three business girls, and thus our mother made a living for herself and us in her widowhood.

Early one Sunday morning she heard a voice which said to her: *"Take the children to the Church of England Sunday School."* Believing God had spoken she obediently took us up the hill to All Saints Church of England at Petersham.

Miss Neill, an elderly Sunday school teacher fell and broke her hip, and our mother helped her to pack up her house to move into a nursing home. In gratitude, Miss Neill gave her some of her treasured books. Sitting on the floor in front of the bookcase at eleven years of age I read in one of Miss Neill's books, entitled "Heroes of the Faith," the story of Mary Slessor. As a child Mary was afraid of cows, but when she grew up she became a missionary and went to Africa, where she was afraid of neither lions nor warring tribesmen.

I immediately identified with Mary, because I too was afraid of cows. Not long afterwards our neighbour Miss Pearson asked me, "What are you going to be when you grow up, Josie?" "A missionary," I replied without hesitation. She passed on the information to my mother, who remembered Hannah in the Bible who gave her son Samuel to the Lord to be his servant. My mother then prayed and gave me to the Lord to be his servant if it should be his will. She did not tell me until after I grew up.

When I was fourteen years old, Dr Paul White, the "Jungle Doctor," visited our church. As he described the sufferings of babies in Tanganyika, East Africa, where witch doctors grew a long fingernail with which to scratch the throats of sick babies, I listened with horror. I said in my heart, "When I grow up I want to be a doctor or a nurse, and go to Tanganyika and stop them from doing that to babies!"

A year later, as autumn leaves chased each other in the wind, I stood listening for the sound of footsteps inside our minister's house. I was fifteen, and confirmation lectures had so inspired me that I wanted to tell our minister of my desire to become a missionary.

"Good morning, Josie. What can I do for you?" Mr Adams asked as he opened the door.

"I want to be a missionary," I told him. He invited me into the hall, while he disappeared into his study. "Give this to your mother and ask her to take you to see these two missionary societies," he said when he came out, handing me a letter.

My mother took me. At the first place the priest advised me to study hard at school if I wanted to be a missionary when I grew up. At the second, the Church Missionary Society, the minister who interviewed us said the same thing, but added, "Let's have a word of prayer before you go." He then prayed that God would lead me in the years ahead, so that if this thing was from him, he would bring it to pass. Tears pricked my closed eyelids as he prayed, for I'd never heard anyone pray for me before, and the experience moved me deeply.

Not long afterwards I took to school the figure of a girl I had modelled out of back-yard clay, and my teacher took it to the headmistress who was so impressed that she arranged for me to sit for an art scholarship. Thus I was directed into a three-year art course at East Sydney Technical College, and I forgot all about being a missionary.

But God did not forget. The words that had come into my mind that day at Pokolbin which had changed the course of my life I now believed to have come from the Holy Spirit of God, and ten years later I was a trained nurse, and had been brought to trust in Jesus Christ as my Saviour.

How I would know if God should call me I didn't know, but of one thing I was sure. God knew how to make me sure, and I should prepare myself by training in obstetrics, just in case.

Chapter 6

Almost a year later a small, dark haired English sister joined the ward staff, and came into the theatre to assist. We chatted as we cleaned up afterwards. "I'd give anything to work in the theatre all the time, as you do," she sighed enviously.

I looked at her excitedly.

"I've just been waiting for you to come along!" I replied. "I want to do obstetrics."

The doctors for whom I worked were mystified as to how I could give up my position to become a trainee nurse again. "Tell me, Sis," the Senior Registrar asked, "Why are you *really* leaving ?"

"Promise you won't laugh if I tell you?" He promised. "I want to prepare myself in case God calls me to be a missionary," I confessed. As a farewell present, the staff gave me a yellow lamp, "because while you've been with us you've seen the light," one of the doctors said in his farewell speech.

My friends were sceptical. "You won't last!" one prophesied. "You won't be able to take being a junior nurse again." But I was confident. I'd done it before. Nevertheless I was nervous as I waited with another new trainee on the first day to take the lift up to the antenatal ward. The sister-in-charge gave us our duties, but as we walked away, a wild hammering on the gong brought us hurrying back. "Oh, by the way," she drawled, "I forgot to tell you. When I hit that gong, *you come!*"

My first duty was to take twenty-three blood-pressures. It was so long since I'd taken a blood-pressure that I was sure I'd forgotten how to do it. And where was the sphygmo with which to take them? I found the stethoscope but couldn't see the sphyg anywhere, and I wasn't game to ask that gong-hammering sister!

"Where's the sphyg please, Lord?" I whispered urgently.

"Look under the medicine trolley," came the thought.

"I've already looked there," I argued.

"Well, look again."

I looked again, this time lifting a pile of temperature charts, and there, underneath them was the sphygmomanometer.

"Thank you, Lord!" I breathed.

As soon as I started actually doing it, the way to take a blood-pressure came back to me. It was automatic, and soon I was in the swing of things again.

I loved obstetrics. The mechanism of labour was awesome, and I marvelled at God's creation. The twelve months training period galloped past. Late one evening I came off duty very tired and was tempted not to read my Bible or to pray that night. You'll be off duty tomorrow Jo, and you can pray and go to church then, I consoled myself. But my better self raised a warning voice. Be careful. That's the way to backslide. Just a little read and a little prayer and after that you can fall into bed.

Heeding the warning, I knelt down, opened the Bible on the bed in front of me, and began to read. Suddenly God's presence was with me in the room, the same way it had been four years previously. Just as had happened then, the Holy Spirit immersed me in indescribable joy. Tears flowed down my cheeks as I silently worshipped. Then, as suddenly as the experience had come, it had gone again.

God must be speaking to me, I thought. I should read again what I'd been reading when this happened, to find out what God was saying to me. My Bible lay open on the bed where I'd left it, and I began to re-read. It was Luke Chapter 14, where Jesus was telling the story of a man who prepared a great feast and sent his servants to call those who had been invited. Instead of coming, they all began to make excuses. The host was furious and said to his servant,

"Go out quickly to the streets and lanes of the city, and bring in the poor, and maimed, and blind and lame........Go out to the highways and hedges, and compel people to come in, that my house may be filled. For I tell you, none of those men who were invited shall taste my banquet." Luke 14:21-24 RSV

Perhaps God is telling me that I'm not to stay here in Australia where there are churches in every suburb and many people won't even cross the road to go into one, I thought. God might be calling me to go out to a country where there are people who have never had a chance to hear. This might be God calling me to be a missionary. If it is, perhaps he'll confirm it to me in church tomorrow.

I remembered that my friend Sandra was coming to church with me the following day. It would be the first time she'd been to church since she'd come to understand what it meant to be saved by Jesus, and not by her own good works. It would be interesting to see how God might give her, a new Christian, and me, feeling called to full time service, a special message each in the same sermon I thought.

At St Barnabas Church, or "Barney's," as we affectionately called it, our regular minister, Dr Howard Guinness, was away on long service leave, and someone I'd never seen before, the Rev Ron Hickin, was preaching that day. He based his sermon on Exodus 21:1-6.

A Hebrew slave could not serve his master for longer than six years. God stipulated that in the seventh year he must go out, free. But if his master had given him a wife and he loved her and his master, he could stay. But if he stayed in the seventh year, he must stay and serve his master for the rest of his life. His ear was bored through with an awl as a mark of voluntary servitude, to show that he chose to belong to his master.

"This is a two part sermon," Mr Hickin said. "The first part is for anyone who has recently come to trust in Jesus as their Saviour. The message to you is that there are happy and unhappy Christians. The happy ones live their lives for Jesus, because Jesus gave his life for them. The unhappy ones try to serve Christ and themselves too. They have divided loyalties and can never be fully happy."

"The second part of the sermon," he said, "is for anyone who has known Christ for some time and has tasted of the things of the Lord and found them good, and now feels that God is calling them to a step which will bind them to him in life-long service.

If such a person is in the church today," he declared, "I want to tell you that I remember the little suburban church where I sat and heard my call to the ministry. If I'm speaking to such a person today, don't have any doubt. This is it! This is the call! This is God's call to you."

We sang the final hymn, and Mr Hickin pronounced the Benediction. Slowly the congregation filed out of the church and stood around in little groups, talking. I stood apart by myself, thinking over the words I had just heard. They confirmed to me that the Lord had indeed spoken to me through his word the night before, and again now. I could never have any doubt but that God had called me to be a missionary, and that for life.

Gradually I became conscious of the dull roar of traffic passing by on the road outside the church gates, and it reminded me that there was a city out there, and that there were cities in all the countries of the world. To which country was God taking me, I wondered?

Chapter 7

What should be the first step, I wondered? I asked God to show me. The thought came to go to St Andrew's Cathedral the following Sunday.

There were Boy Scouts everywhere, and I found that it was a special Service for Scouts. The sermon was based on the Apostle Paul's letter to a young man named Timothy, and the New Testament Lesson was from the old King James Version of the Bible:

"Study to show thyself approved unto God, a workman that needeth not to be ashamed, rightly dividing the word of truth." 2 *Timothy 2:15 AV*

The Scouts, and indeed all of us, were encouraged to study the Bible so that we would gain wisdom from God, and be able to teach others also.

God has shown me the next step, I thought. It means I should go to Bible School. Which one should I go to? I asked the new minister at St Barnabas who had been a missionary in China, the Rev Roger Bowie. "Deaconess House, Moore College," he replied, "just around the corner from your hospital." (Deaconess House is now known as Mary Andrews College.)

A small, dark-haired woman answered the door-bell and introduced herself as Mary Andrews, the principal. Her brown eyes were welcoming, and she had a humble, friendly manner. She invited me into her study and as we talked she told me that she had done her nursing training at the same psychiatric hospital at which I'd trained. After that she'd gone as a missionary to China.

Within an hour it was all arranged. I was enrolled for the two year diploma course, due to start in the new year, just two months away. My fees would be covered by two days work each week in the parish of Kensington. I thanked God, but still had one problem. Who would pay my mother's electricity bills? I had always done this for her, and now I would have no salary. I asked God to somehow provide for her.

In the Nurses' Home the telephone rang in the hall. It was Bill, my brother-in-law, with a surprising proposition to make. He and my sister would sell their house and my mother would sell hers, and they would buy a two-storey house and live together again. I was delighted.

"Clermont," a two-storey white house with a beautiful garden became ours. There was a circular driveway with a cypress pine in the centre, which Bill would adorn with coloured lights at Christmas. A giant cactus that only bloomed in the moonlight grew on one side of the front door, and on the other side was a camellia garden of snowy white and pink blossoms. A wisteria arch, a port-wine magnolia, freesias, jonquils, daffodils, forget-me-nots, roses and violets that all bloomed in their season made up the rest of the garden. There were also many green, shady trees. It was the most beautiful garden we'd ever had.

As I'd only be home on Saturdays I claimed the smallest room, from which a ladder went up to the roof. From there the view extended eastward to the Harbour Bridge and the ocean, and westward to the Blue Mountains There was room in the house for my mother to have a boarder, a young man named Bev, and I didn't need to contribute to electricity bills!

Moore College and Deaconess House students had lectures together. I liked New Testament lectures best, which were laced with the whimsical humour of Dr Alan Cole. In the second year New Testament lectures were made both lively and profound by the devout and dramatic presentation of the Rev Marcus Loane (who later became Bishop and then Archbishop)

There were also lessons to be learnt by living together, and visiting speakers shared their experience with us. Mrs Vera Langford-Smith, wife of a missionary bishop in Kenya, described in her quiet and tranquil manner what happens when someone gets an eyelash in their eye.

"Your whole body loses its peace," she commented. "It's only a tiny thing, but until you get it out you can't go on. Friction among those with whom we live and work is like an eyelash irritating the eye, and we need to deal with it, or God's work will suffer." I never forgot her lesson, but many years later I would have to learn it in a way that I didn't like.

When the two years ended, I was still as sure as ever of my missionary vocation, but I'd lost confidence in my ability as a midwife. Needing more experience, I first signed up for a four months Tresillian Course. Jan Byrne, a fellow student, helped me with my weakest subject, decimal calculations for premature baby feeds. Jan and I became life-long friends.

Next I obtained a job at South Sydney Women's Hospital which provided excellent labour-ward experience. My mother, now in her sixties, wanted to move nearer to our church, St Anne's Ryde. It meant having her own house again, and she found a fibro cottage in the same street as St Anne's Sunday School, with bus and shops just around the corner. I determined to pay off the small mortgage for her before going overseas. When the final payment had been made, I felt free to apply to a missionary society. Which one? Since no specific guidance had come from God, the appropriate one seemed to be that of my own church. Very excited at having made a decision, I hurried up the stairs of CMS, the mission I'd been directed to as a fifteen year old girl. A highly respected elderly lady, Miss Peach* was helping at the reception desk that day.

"Yes my dear, what can I do for you?" she asked.

Suddenly I didn't know what to say. I stood looking blankly at her, struggling to put into words the thing that was so dear to my heart.

"Can I help you?" she repeated.

"I - I've come!" I stuttered.

"Yes, my dear; I can see that you've come. But what for?"

Plucking up my courage, I announced, "I've come to apply."

"To apply for *what?*" she asked, mystified.

Honestly! I thought. Isn't this a missionary society? What does she mean- *"for what?"* Taking a deep breath, I said plainly, "To be a missionary."

Miss Peach threw back her head and laughed. My expression must have been a study. What a reaction to this sacred moment!

"What's the matter?" I asked, astonished.

"My dear," she gasped, trying to control her laughter, "You'd be no good as a missionary!"

My amazement knew no bounds, "Why not?" I asked, completely mystified.

"Oh, my dear," she said, starting to laugh again, "You're far too thin*!"

Later it seemed to be funny, but that day it didn't seem to be the least bit funny. I didn't even recognise that it was like a re-play of the reaction of the matron at the mental hospital when I'd applied to work there several years previously. but my reaction was the same.

"I'd like a set of application papers, please," I said firmly.

Wiping the tears of mirth from her eyes, Miss Peach found a set of application papers and passed them across the counter. Thanking her, I put them into my handbag, and walked back down the stairs with far less assurance than I'd bounded up them. Would she be able to influence others against accepting me, I wondered? On the way home I called in to see my former minister, the Rev John Reid, and asked for his urgent prayers. "Don't worry, Jo," he said consolingly. "If God has really called you, nothing will be able to stop you."

I later heard that Miss Peach had felt called to missionary service when she was young, and ill health had prevented her from going overseas. Instead, God had used her in his work here at home, where she inspired many young people to give their lives to God's service, both at home and overseas.

Being thin did not threaten my acceptance as a missionary candidate, but something else did. For some time I'd found that bending over to deliver babies put a severe strain on my back. Neither prayers at St Andrew's Cathedral Healing Services nor the physiotherapy ordered by the CMS doctor made any difference, my back still hurt. I couldn't understand. Why, if God had called me, didn't he heal me so that I could go?

"Missionary societies don't usually accept people after the age of thirty," people warned me, "It gets more difficult to learn a new language as you get older." My thirty-second birthday came and went, and I began to worry.

Each year at Katoomba CMS held a week long conference known as "Summer School," and for the first time I went. The Rev Ken Short spoke on Caleb, a mighty man of God in the Old Testament. Caleb said:

"I am this day eighty-five years old. I am still as strong to this day as I was in the day that Moses sent me; my strength now is as my strength was then, for war, and for going and coming." Joshua 14:10-12 RSV

I stopped worrying about my age.

Almost a year after my original application I walked along Macquarie Street for yet another medical checkup. Outside St Stephen's Presbyterian Church on the notice board was printed:

"Having done all ......stand"   Ephesians 6:13 RSV

I stood there, thinking, I've done all I can and there's nothing more I can do. *"Stand"* must mean to stand and wait. I'll have to wait for God to do something.

My watch told me there was time before my appointment to go into the church and pray. Inside, the traffic of the city was muted. As I quietly entered and sat down, I saw on the book rest in front of me a small card with a reproduction of an old painting on it. It depicted Dr Livingstone, the famous missionary doctor who explored Africa, kneeling in yellow sunburnt grass attending to a sick African boy who lay on the ground, his head and shoulders cradled in his mother's arms, while the doctor held a small glass of medicine to his lips. The figure of the Lord Jesus in white light could be dimly seen standing behind the doctor. Under the picture was printed:

"Having done all,...stand."

The picture became one of my most treasured possessions.

That day the doctor seemed to be more discouraging than ever. He mentioned a possible diagnosis, and told me to return again in another three months. On the way home I went into a second hand bookshop, found a medical book and looked up the disease he had mentioned. It was a degenerative disease, and if this should be my problem I would end up in a wheel chair, and finally be bedridden. More mystified than ever, I walked down the street in the rain, wondering, "Why?" If God has called me, why don't I get better, so I can go? For the first time I considered the possibility that, even though God had called me, perhaps it might be to give and pray for others who went, and not to go myself.

Jean Parr, a missionary nurse who had to come home from Tanganyika because of ill health, gave me a small book, and I determined to spend the afternoon reading it. It was *Dying to Live* by Jessie Penn Lewis.

"How deep is the death of Christ to go in us?" Jessie asked. "How deep shall the sword of the Cross cut into our lives? Shall it touch....your ambitions? It is not so much your getting victory over these things, as your death to them, in the death of Christ, that is important."

I'd known that we were to consider ourselves dead to sin, but it had never occurred to me that we might be asked to die to something good. For instance, our ambition to serve God! What if God wanted me to serve him in some other way than I wanted? Was I willing for that? I saw that Jesus didn't cling to his own life, but gave it up because that is what his Father wanted him to do, and that we also must be prepared to serve God in the way he wants, which may not necessarily be the way we want. That afternoon I relinquished what had become my dearest ambition. With tears, I prayed a prayer of acceptance, trying to follow Jesus' example.

"Lord, I accept your will, whatever it is. If you want me to go overseas I'm ready to go, but if you want me to serve you from the home end I accept that instead. Let your will, not mine, be done."

The battle over, I found new peace in trusting God to do whatever was best. One week later a letter arrived for me from CMS. I opened it eagerly, and read:

"We have been informed by the doctor that your back is no better. However, since it is no worse, and we have an acute shortage of nurses, we have decided to accept you as a missionary candidate."

I'd learnt that God's delays are not denials. He has much to teach us in our waiting times. Faith in his call is tried by discouragements and is proven to be real when it remains strong. God had been waiting for me to be willing to accept his will, whatever that was, and I'd learnt that if God has really called us he will open the door when the right time comes.

Many years later I would understand why God would not allow me to go overseas until I had first begun to learn this important principle of relinquishment, for the time would come when I would have to relinquish what I loved the most and submit to God, and it would dash my world to pieces.

45

** Miss Peach – not her real name*

Chapter 8

"Which country do you feel God is calling you to?" the Committee asked, when the day of my interview came. I searched my mind but came up with no answer. "Maybe to South America, or Malaya," I replied, "but to be honest, I really don't know. I only know that God has called me to be a missionary."

"Well, if you don't know, we've prayed about it," a committee member said, "and we believe that God wants you to go to Tanganyika."

I sat in stunned silence. Tanganyika! The place of my childhood dreams! From the dim past, I heard Dr Paul White describe babies having their throats traumatised by a cruel fingernail, and I heard myself say in my heart, "When I grow up, I want to be a doctor or a nurse and go to Tanganyika, and stop them from doing that to babies." Now it was coming true.

"Let's have a word of prayer before you go," someone suggested.

This was the second time I'd been prayed for in that place. The minister who had interviewed me there eighteen years before had said the same thing – "*Let's have a word of prayer before you go.*" He'd prayed that if this thing was from God, he would bring it to pass. Now that prayer was being answered.

My interview was ended. As I travelled home in the bus, I reflected on what I had thought was only a childhood dream, and it was difficult to believe it was real. I wanted to pray and ask God if it was really he and not just the committee sending me to Tanganyika, but I knew I was too tired to ask such a momentous question that night. I would wait till the morning. On my arrival home my mother and I hugged each other.

"Well?" she asked. "What did the Committee say?"

"Tanganyika," I replied. It must have come as a shock to her, for Africa seemed so far away, and she was already in her sixties. But if so she hid her dismay in her usual practical manner. "Well, come and wash your hands and come to the table. I have a nice baked dinner ready for you."

After dinner I went to my room. There was only one piece of mail for me, an issue of the Christian nurses' magazine I subscribed to. I'll pray about Tanganyika in the morning, I thought. I'm too tired tonight, but I'll just look through this. An article on the first page caught my attention. It was entitled *Black Diamond,* and told of an uncut diamond that was a priceless gem, not yet mined, waiting somewhere in Africa to be found, destined for the King's crown. If I were to find just one black diamond for Jesus in Africa, it would be worth while going there for, I thought as I drifted off to sleep.

My Scripture Union Bible reading next morning was Joshua 5:12-15. The manna of the desert ceased, for Joshua was about to enter the promised land. Suddenly he saw before him a man standing there. Who was he? Was he on their side, or the enemies, Joshua asked? Neither, the man replied. He had come as the Commander of the Lord's forces, and he told Joshua to take his shoes off, for he was standing on holy ground.

Joshua knew what that meant, for when God had visited Moses he had told him to take off his shoes, for the place where he was standing was holy. *(Genesis 3:1-6)* Joshua removed his sandals and worshipped, for he knew, then, it was the Lord himself. And I had the answer to my question. I believed that it was not just the committee sending me to Africa, it was the Lord himself.

———•••———

On the sixth of March, 1962, coloured paper streamers twisted and billowed in the sea-breeze, tugging at passengers' fingers as they lined the rail of the white ship *Strathmore*. I was among them. Down on the wharf where relatives and friends held the other end of the streamers I could see my mother and sister and her husband and their three little children, and many of my friends. It warmed my heart that they all had come to say goodbye. At 7pm, unannounced, the distance between the ship and the wharf began slowly to widen. The ship was moving. Although it had been expected, it came as a shock to me. Dear faces quickly became indistinguishable, and within minutes the wharf was left behind, like a tiny island being swallowed up by the approaching night.

My brother-in-law had promised that they would drive to the point of land under the Harbour Bridge and flash their car lights as we passed. I stood at the rail, knowing that two of the many beams criss-crossing the darkening water were theirs. As the majestic ship passed beneath the Bridge it sent out two deep-throated hoots. My sister wrote later that to her it was the saddest sound she had ever heard. It seemed as if I were going out of their lives forever.

For me, it was the fulfilment of something that stretched back to the day I was born, and stretched forward into the unknown future.

Marjie and Jo, 10 years later (1972)

For my mother it was her offering of me to the Lord. He had offered his Son for her, and she was giving me to God. In the front of the Bible she had given me she had written some words quoted from a well known hymn:

Were the whole realm of nature mine,
That were an offering far too small;
Love so amazing, so divine
Demands my soul, my life, my all.

All night long the ship sailed down the eastern coast of Australia. Each time I awoke, I could hear the heavy throb of the engines, making the ship shudder, and the sound of water churning past the porthole. Each time the same thought came to me,

"It's not the ship, it's God's hand bearing me along, carrying me to Africa."

Next morning I wrote my first letter to my mother, and told her about the thought that had come to me so insistently throughout my first night at sea. My mother's first letter to me, and mine to her, crossed, and I received hers in Melbourne at the same time as she received mine in Sydney. I tore her letter open eagerly.

"After the ship sailed," she had written," we went home, and I went to bed. At about two o'clock in the morning I woke up, and as I woke, I saw a vision of God's hand, so big that it filled the bedroom, shining with light, and right down in his palm was the little white ship, *Strathmore*. The vision slowly faded as I woke."

As I read her letter and she read mine, we knew that God had assured us both that it was indeed God who was taking me to Africa.

Dorothy Brennan at 67 soon after Jo left for Africa

Chapter 9

For five weeks the immense ocean, the sky, and the brilliant stars gave us unlimited joy. The journey would be my only one by sea, for the day of the great ocean liners was about to be displaced by the jet age. For four days between Perth and Colombo there were no waves at all, and the Indian Ocean looked like a giant pond. Cumulus clouds stood on the horizon, reflected in the water. Only flying fish broke the surface, shattering it in showers of silver as they leapt in the shadow of the travelling ship. Behind us, a foaming wake stretched out like a track forever disappearing as it mingled again with the ocean, reminding me of a picture of the sea which I had at home, with a verse printed on it: *Thy way is in the sea, and thy path in the great waters, and thy footsteps are not known Psalm 77:19 AV*

There were six adults and three children in our party. Seven more adults and four children would join us at language school. All adults seemed to be university graduates, most of them doctors and teachers. It didn't occur to me to wonder how I would keep up with such "intelligentsia" in the language school, since I had left school at fifteen and had never studied another language!

One unforgettable dawn we awoke to find the ship berthed in Dar-es-Salaam, capital of Tanganyika. After five weeks at sea one of the children insisted on calling their large family room in the hotel their "cabin." The following day we boarded a train for Dodoma, in the central region. At two o'clock in the morning a loud banging on the compartment doors jolted us awake. Pulling on some clothes, I stumbled out into the soft, sultry night air of Morogoro. In the starlight, a tall figure was moving along the platform from person to person, speaking to each of us individually. It was Alf Stanway, the Australian Bishop of Central Tanganyika. He happened to be in Morogoro and thought he'd come down to the train to welcome his new missionaries.

"You must be Jo," he said, giving me a warm handshake. "You'll be going to a sixty-bed hospital at Berega, and after a year you'll be going to Murgwanza."

Berega - Murgwanza! Berega - Murgwanza! the train wheels seemed to say as they clacked over the wooden sleepers on the track, recording the unfamiliar names on my memory. I awoke again with a start. The train was standing still, this time at Dodoma. It was 6am, and a group of people were already on the station welcoming us and whisking us away to various homes for breakfast. I was taken to the home of the secretary of the diocese, Margaret McKechnie. That afternoon I was driven, with teachers Dick and Judy and their children, thirty miles through a range of hills to Mvumi. Pink and white frangipani trees lined the road of the last hill, where we turned off the road under a baobab tree festooned with bougainvillea, and stopped beside a long mud and concrete house. This was to be our home for the next three months.

Crows were cawing in the baobab trees as we all filed into the primary school on Monday morning. Squeezing ourselves into the child-sized desks, we paid attention as our language teacher, Lionel Bakewell, introduced us to the man who would open the language school. He was Daudi, a qualified teacher who was chaplain to the hospital. As he tapped his way in with a stick, we saw that he was blind. Daudi's sensitive fingers moved rapidly across the page of his Braille Bible as he read to us in excellent English. He read of how Jesus called Peter three times to tend his sheep, then prophesied the kind of death Peter would die to glorify God. Peter immediately turned and looked at John. *"Lord, what about this man?"* he asked.

Jesus replied, *"If it is my will that he remain until I come, what is that to you? Follow me!" John 21:21,22 RSV*

"You've all come here to learn Swahili." Daudi said. "Some of you will learn quickly, others more slowly. Jesus' words to Peter give us a warning not to look at others. Look only to Jesus, who has called you here." If I'd taken to heart Daudi's message I could have saved myself a lot of suffering, but I didn't. At the end of two weeks we were given a test, and as a result Lionel divided us into two groups, the fast and the slow. The carpenter and I comprised the slow class, and when he unexpectedly left I was alone in my class.

"Don't be discouraged, Jo." Lionel said. "Even though you're slow at first, in the end, you'll get it." No, I'll never learn this language, it's impossible, I thought. Faith, the hospital sister who shared our house, allowed me to use her sitting room for my early morning quiet times. In its seclusion I shed many tears. Why has God brought me to this country if I can't learn the language, I wept. I prayed desperately for God to help me.

One morning as I walked across the room that I shared with Coralie, a searing pain shot through my foot. "Something's bitten me!" I gasped. Coralie ran to Faith, who called Joe Taylor, the medical superintendent. He came down armed with a syringe of local anaesthetic and injected it into the bite. Faith searched the floor and found the culprit – a small brown scorpion, which she promptly dispatched. A few days later I came to the place in my Bible where Jesus told his disciples as he sent them out, *"I have given you authority to tread upon serpents and scorpions, and over all the power of the enemy; and nothing shall hurt you." Luke 10:19 RSV*

"But it *did* hurt, Lord!" I exclaimed, puzzled. "More than anything else has ever hurt me!" I came to the conclusion that Jesus' words must have some other, deeper meaning than the physical. "What does it mean, Lord?" I asked. A question flashed into my mind: *"What is hurting you more than anything else at this moment?"* That's easy! I responded. Being bottom of the language school! *"Then it won't harm you."* came the reply. Insight suddenly came. I'd been suffering from intellectual pride, and it had been pricked. That was what was hurting so much! But the question still remained, how could I work in a hospital when I couldn't understand the language?

Coralie and I attended an African fellowship meeting and Stanley, a brother in Christ, translated for us. We read from the book of Jonah, who cried out to God from the belly of the great fish, *"The waters closed in over me, the deep was round about me; weeds were wrapped about my head" Jonah 2:5 RSV.* That's exactly how Swahili makes me feel, I thought, like seaweed wrapped around my head.

"But I with the voice of thanksgiving will sacrifice to thee; what I have vowed I will pay. Deliverance belongs to the Lord! And the Lord spoke to the fish, and it vomited out Jonah upon the dry land. Jonah 2:6;9;10 RSV .

For the first time I noticed that it was *before* the fish vomited Jonah out that Jonah gave thanks to God for saving him! Jonah believed while he was still down there. After he believed and thanked God, the fish vomited him out upon the dry land.

I decided to follow Jonah's example and believe while I was still down there. Even though Swahili was still like weeds wrapped around my head, I now believed that one day, in God's time, I would be able to speak. The first step of progress came when an African staff nurse went for walks with me in the evening so that I could practise conversation. I confessed to her my greatest fear: that should a woman have a history of previous still-birth I might not understand what she was saying, and this could have very serious consequences. So as Mariamu and I walked we did a little role-play. Mariamu was the staff-nurse, I was the pregnant mother. She inquired about my previous pregnancies.

"Wa kwanza?" she asked (meaning my first pregnancy.)

"Alikufa kabla alipozaliwa" she taught me to say. He died before he was born. I repeated it carefully after her.

"Wa pili?" (the second) ...."Alikufa kabla alipozaliwa."

"Wa tatu?""(the third)" ...."Alikufa kabla alipozaliwa."

By the time I'd reached my ninth still-birth, tears of mirth were running down Mariamu's cheeks, and I was beginning to feel I'd got the phrase. "How do I say "he lived?" I inquired.

"Yu hai" Mariamu choked. "He's alive!"

"Yu hai." I repeated. "Yu hai, yu hai, yu hai! "

I'd discovered a way in which I could learn Swahili, by simply repeating it, as a child does. Once I mastered a phrase I could dissect and analyse it by looking it up in the grammar book.

God was answering my prayer, and although I didn't know it, before my first furlough I would pass all my language exams.

Chapter 10

The sound of the departing car faded into the distance. I walked through the empty ten-roomed house to my own small room at the end, where I knelt down and burst into tears. It was two weeks since I'd arrived, and the doctor, Ken, and his wife Allison had left to return their children to school after the holidays, taking with them Betty, the nurse I'd come to replace. Enid, my house-mate had already left on a Mothers' Union safari and they'd all be away for a week or more. I'd known they were going but it didn't hit me until the car drove away that I'd be the only white person left at Berega, and the realisation gave me an initial shock of loneliness. When I could stop crying, I opened my Bible, and my gaze fell upon these words:

"This day is holy to the Lord your God; do not mourn or weep." For all the people wept when they heard the words of the law. Then he said to them, "Go your way, eat the fat and drink sweet wine and send portions to him for whom nothing is prepared; for this day is holy to our Lord; do not be grieved, for the joy of the Lord is your strength." Nehemiah 8:9-10 RSV

God was speaking to me through his word, telling me not to weep because this was a special day to the Lord for me. He'd brought me to this place to help share the gospel with needy people, and I was not to be sad. The joy of the Lord was my strength. I got up and walked up to the hospital, and the joy of the Lord filled my heart.

As well as the Wakaguru people, many Masai came to

the hospital. The women flapped around the ward in long, cow-hide garments. Tiny coloured beads formed their ornaments, sewn into coronets for their shaven heads, enormous rings for their ears, and intricate necklaces. Brass bangles sheathed their slim arms and legs.

It was not unusual to find a row of long hunting spears, tips embedded in the earth, outside our house, while their owners sat along the verandah listening to gospel records in their own language. Jesus' parable of the lost sheep was their favourite. The plaintive ba-a-a of a sheep followed by the distant howl of a hyena was so real that it never failed to bring a laugh of recognition.

At night the cots in the children's ward were all empty as mothers spread their garments on the floor and took their babies down to lie beside them. Mwendwa, our senior staff-nurse, had been born a twin at a time when twins were "an endangered species" in Wakaguru culture. She'd been rescued and brought up by an Australian CMS nurse, Margery Paull. Mwendwa was now a tower of strength to many, including me.

Hodi! Sister! Kichwa mlangoni! the night nurse called at my bedroom door a few weeks later. "Do you know what she's saying?" Enid called out from her room nearby. "Yes," I replied, rapidly pulling on my uniform. *"Kichwa mlangoni* ... the head is at the door ... the baby's head's on view!" I was needed in labour ward.

Slowly I was beginning to pick up a few Swahili phrases, but when Enid tried to help me with some formal Swahili lessons she despaired. "I only taught you that yesterday," she would groan. "I'm sorry, I've forgotten," was all I could say. We laughed together and we cried together, and finally we agreed that we would stop the lessons. I would have to learn at my own pace. I loved to escape the Swahili speaking world at the end of each day and go for a walk with Enid where we could converse in our own language.

"I think it would be a good idea if we went for separate walks," Enid said one evening, explaining that after she'd spent all day in the office she liked a long, brisk walk to stretch her legs. "If we go for separate walks it will give me a longer walk and give you more time to stand and look at the sunset," she said reasonably.

That night I went outside under a tree to have a private cry. Except for the doctor and his wife there were no other Europeans at Berega, and Allison had made it clear the first time we met that we should make our own friends amongst the Africans, and not cling to each other. Was Enid trying to encourage me to spend more time getting to know African people, I wondered? "I don't know enough Swahili yet to make African friends, Lord," I wept. "Please don't let Enid give up our walks together! "

Unexpectedly a trip to Mvumi materialised. "You go," said Enid generously. "I get out on Mothers' Union trips, but you haven't been away since you got here three months ago."

What fun it was to unpack in the pretty guest room of the sisters' house at Mvumi where my hostess, Genevieve, lived. I renewed my friendship with Coralie, the lab assistant with whom I'd shared a room at language school. "It's only six months till our first year holidays." she reminded me. "Let's go together!" She had a friend working at the Machame Lutheran Hospital on the slopes of Mt Kilimanjaro, and suggested that we visit her, and also visit May Dobson, a retired missionary living in Kenya. That afternoon there was a meeting of the African Revival Fellowship, and Coralie and I went. Stanley, an African health worker, translated for us while I read from my English Bible.

Thus says the Lord:"Cursed is the man who trusts in man, and makes flesh his arm, whose heart turns away from the Lord. He is like a shrub in the desert, and shall not see any good come.

Blessed is the man who trusts in the Lord ... He is like a tree planted by water, that sends out its roots by the stream, and does not fear when heat comes, for its leaves remain green, and is not anxious in the year of drought, for it does not cease to bear fruit." Jeremiah 17:5-8 RSV

For the first time I recognised that I'd been leaning on Enid, and that if I wanted to be a blessing in this new country I must lean only upon God. If Enid wanted to give up our evening walks together I was ready now to accept it.

On arrival back at Berega I found that we'd had an addition to our household. Someone had given Enid a puppy! He was a fox terrier, and she named him Raca, Swahili for Spot, because he had a black patch over one eye. What a difference Raca made, entertaining us with his escapades, particularly on our evening walks! The same old road became new for us as Enid rescued her puppy from getting hung up on roots and from tumbling over rocks. We laughed at his antics, and while Enid raced with Raca, I had time to stand and gaze at the sunset! God had answered my prayers – through the gift of a puppy.

Enid took me to visit her African friends, Mama Sala and Mama Damari, and they became my friends too. Mama Sala invited me to her little thatched house to learn to converse in Swahili. She spoke slowly and clearly, and I repeated phrases after her. At home, African visitors came frequently to talk with Enid, and recurring phrases gradually became recognisable to me. At my own pace and in my own way, I was learning the language.

At the end of our first year, Coralie and I flew to Nairobi in an MAF *(Missionary Aviation Fellowship)* plane. It seemed hard to believe that only two hours after leaving Tanzania we were sitting down to an evening meal in Kenya.

Chapter 11

Smiling grey eyes and a gentle manner made May Dobson still beautiful in her mature years. An Australian, she was a qualified teacher as well as a certificated nurse, and had come to Tanganyika in 1932 to train nurses for a tiny bush hospital at Mvumi in central Tanganyika. She showed us an age-worn tract printed in 1928 (the year I was born) appealing for a doctor for Mvumi hospital, the nearest medical help being approximately three hundred miles away in Dar-es-Salaam. But when May got to Mvumi she found there were no educated girls for her to train. Switching roles to her teaching profession, she commenced Mvumi Girls' School. Eight years later her first pupils passed their standard eight exams, and were ready to start training to be nurses. Over the years, thousands of girls passed through Mvumi Girls' School, and qualified nurses went out from Mvumi to staff clinics and hospitals all over Tanganyika.

Coralie and I enjoyed May's gracious company, and we revelled in the contrasts we found in the Kinangop hills. Roses in her garden seemed to be the size of dinner plates. In the daytime it was quite hot, being only fifty miles from the equator, yet in her cosy sitting room at night it was cold enough to enjoy a log fire. We climbed nearby Elephant Mountain which rose 8,000 feet above sea level, and beside the path we found forget-me-nots.

Our time with May came to an end, and soon we were in a bus speeding back across the Nairobi game park. In the Machame Lutheran Hospital's small guest lodge on the slopes of Mount Kilimanjaro, I woke early the next morning

61

and went outside. Walking through the dew-wet garden, I turned around, looked back and up, and caught my breath in wonder. A wooden cross on top of the lodge was silhouetted against the snow-capped dome of Mount Kilimanjaro, gleaming in the rising sun. The base of the mountain was invisible, and the white dome seemed suspended on blue mist. Hurrying back inside, I called Coralie to come and see the mountain before it disappeared behind the clouds again.

But it didn't disappear. For the next four mornings the mountain remained "out" until midday. Coralie visited local people while I painted a picture of the mountain. On the last day a little African boy herded his goats under the shade of a thorn-tree in the centre of the green field where I sat, and with a few strokes of the brush I put him in. The picture was complete, ready to take home in three years' time as a gift for my mother.

Back in Dodoma Coralie and I said goodbye, and returned to our respective hospitals. A shock awaited me at Berega. In the interests of nationalisation the smaller hospitals were no longer to have white A-grade sisters in charge. Now the doctor was the only boss, and sisters would work alongside B-grade African staff nurses. Like them, I would have my own ward to care for.

I'd watched the staff nurses madly pumping up primus stoves used for sterilising, with kerosene-fed flames ascending. Now it would be my turn to pump madly with flames ascending! Would I manage to light the primus? I woke in the early morning worrying about it.

Our pastor, Gresford, customarily held a small evening meeting for prayer in the church, and I went along. He spoke about the giants mentioned in the Bible. Moses sent twelve spies ahead into Canaan to spy out the promised land. Ten spies came back with a bad report. They said: *"there we saw the giants, the sons of Anak......We were in our own sight as grasshoppers."* Numbers 13:33 AV (abbreviated) Because they saw giants, they were afraid to enter the land God had promised to give them.

Satan still frightens us with giants, Gresford said. Satan blows up our fears to giant size, like blowing up a balloon. As he spoke I could see Satan standing behind my bed in the early hours of the morning, saying "Whooooo! You won't be able to light the primus! It will burst into flames!"

I laughed. Of course I could do it! With God's help, I could do anything I was asked to do. Now that I recognised my enemy, I refused to be intimidated.

How happy I was looking after premature babies, labour-ward cases, and the mothers and babies of the maternity ward, instead of checking lanterns and kerosene and looking after the drug store. The administrative tasks I gladly gave to the African Staff Nurses and they liked their new responsibility.

I began to get to know the nurses. Mariamu was a pastor's daughter who was working to pay her school fees and complete standard eight. She then hoped to train as a nurse at Mvumi. One night she called me outside to listen. "Ugh, ugh, ugh" went the sound. *"Simba!"* Mariamu whispered, her eyes big. "Lion! Come inside!" I wasted no time in hurrying in and closing the door.

Enid's furlough was approaching. "I'm worried about you" she said. "I don't like leaving you alone."

"Don't worry," I told her. "I'll be all right."

After Enid had gone, Raca became my faithful companion and watch-dog. I thanked God for him, but there was one problem. How was I going to bath him? He hated baths, and if I even *thought* the word 'bath' he seemed to know! One hot day I quietly crept around and closed all the doors while he was snoozing on the mat, and he didn't notice until it was too late. The smell of disinfectant must have wakened him, and before I could attach a rope to his collar he was up and off, racing around the house trying to escape. Realising he was trapped, he ran and hid under my bed. Every time I tried to get him out, I was met by fierce growls.

I had to work out a way to bath Raca or put up with the fleas. Suddenly I saw a way. The floor was made of concrete, so water wouldn't harm it. Removing the mattress, I climbed onto the iron frame of my bed with the bucket of dog-wash in my hand, and with one swift movement I emptied the lot through the wire springs on top of the cringing dog beneath. Yelping wildly, Raca raced out, shaking himself all over the bedroom. I opened the door and he fled, to roll in the dirt outside.

I gave a sigh of relief. Brief as it was, Raca had had his bath.

Chapter 12

There was just time for a quick cup of tea before I went on duty. I lit the kerosene stove. As I did so, a strong urge came upon me to pray. I blew out the flame and returned to my room, but the clock on my dressing-table told me it was only 4.30 pm. There's time to pray and have a cup of tea as well, I thought. Returning to the kitchen, I re-lit the stove. But again the urge to pray came so strongly that for a second time I blew out the flame and went to my room. As I knelt down, the responsibility of the hospital came upon me like a great burden, too heavy to bear, for the doctor was away. I cried out to the Lord, and opened my Bible, and the words that I read gave me the strength that I needed.

The Lord is my rock, and my fortress, and my deliverer,

my God, my rock, in whom I take refuge,

my shield, and the horn of my salvation, my stronghold.
Psalm 18:1-2 RSV

As I counted the things that God was to me, my defender, my protector, my strong fortress and my refuge, I also remembered that Jesus is the great physician. My fear subsided as I placed all the patients in his care.

It was five o'clock, time to go on duty. As I walked up towards the hospital I saw a man waiting outside the maternity ward. His daughter was at the bus stand, he told me. They had come on the bus because she was having a baby. Would I please come in the Land Rover and get her?

At the bus stop I found a crowd of women gathered

around the patient, who was lying on the ground. They parted to let me in, and I knelt down beside her and lifted the black cloth she was wearing. Between her thighs lay the body of her dead baby, the head still unborn. She had delivered five hours before. If they'd stayed on the bus they could have reached Kilosa government hospital, sixty miles away, where there was a doctor, but now the bus had gone and there would not be another that night.

I knelt there, wondering what to do. Should I get one of the local shop-keepers to drive her to Kilosa in our Land Rover, or should I attempt to get the baby out? I thought back to a few weeks earlier when we'd had a similar case. The doctor had struggled to deliver an impacted breech but failed. The baby had died while he'd been struggling, and he'd finally extracted the dead infant by using a special instrument.

"What should I do if I get such a case when you're away?" I'd asked. He'd considered for a moment then replied, "You should try to do what you've just seen me do. There'd be no point in subjecting the mother to a sixty mile journey over rough roads if the baby's already dead."

Conscious of the fact that God had prepared me for this emergency by urging me to pray, and that I'd committed the patients into the care of Jesus the great physician, I decided to try to get the baby out, trusting in God for the mother's safety. Back at the hospital both Staff Nurse Mwendwa and I tried to deliver the head, but without success. After giving the mother an anaesthetic I endeavoured to use the instrument the doctor had indicated, but feared to persist lest I sever the head of the dead infant from its body.

"We'll have to send her to Kilosa," I said, giving up, and Mwendwa agreed. The woman woke up to find herself still undelivered, but the anaesthetic had given her a brief respite from labour, and I hoped they might reach the hospital before contractions recommenced. Willing hands laid her on a mattress in the back of the Land Rover. Mwendwa went with her, taking an injection to give if labour recommenced on the way.

The hours seemed long as we waited for news. Late the following day the Land Rover returned. The doctor had tried unsuccessfully to deliver the head, and finally resorted to Caesarean operation. There was a slight rupture in the uterus which he was able to repair, and the patient recovered. How near she'd come to death, I thought, fervently thanking God for watching over her. Any other difficult cases, advised the doctor, should be sent straight to on to him by Land Rover. At that moment we still had a Land Rover, but that was about to change!

One week later I woke early, while it was still dark. A piece of iron hanging from a tree that served as a church bell was being struck in a strange muffled way, with long pauses between each strike. Someone important must have died, I thought, hastily pulling on my clothes. Several lanterns were already making a pool of light on the ground as I joined the people gathering outside the pastor's house. Yohanna Omari, the Church's first African Bishop, a man greatly loved, had died suddenly in a village not far away.

Two days later I allowed our Land Rover to be used to take people to the funeral. There was an accident, and the Land Rover was destroyed. There could be no insurance, for the driver had not been not fully licensed. I had not wanted the vehicle to go, but I'd given in to pressure without personally examining the license of the man who offered to drive. Had I done so I would have seen that it was only a provisional licence, and he should have had a licensed driver with him. Now the hospital had no vehicle. But there was one thing for which I was deeply grateful to God. Although everyone was thrown out onto the road, miraculously no one was seriously hurt.

I wrote to my mother and told her what had happened, and she wrote back that every night before she went to bed it was her custom to look at my photograph beside her bed and say "Good night" before she went to sleep. About the time of our troubles she'd looked at the picture, and although it was a black and white photograph, the eyes seemed to her to be red, as if I'd been crying. She took the photograph and held it under a stronger light. It still looked the same. She took it back to the bedroom and switched on the bedside light. The eyes still looked red and tearful. "Then I knew" she wrote, "that you must be in some terrible trouble, and God must be alerting me to pray. I prayed for you until two o'clock in the morning, and then suddenly the burden lifted, and I knew that God had answered my prayer."

When I read my mother's letter I knew that just as God had alerted me to pray for the safety of the patients when there was a the difficult midwifery case coming, so he had alerted my mother also, thousands of miles away, to pray.

Before leaving home to go out to Africa, in the rush of many things to arrange I'd knelt one morning to pray and it had occurred to me that I needed partners in prayer for the work ahead.

"Lord, do you want me to send letters to people willing to pray?" I'd asked, and God had led me to read this promise:

Call to me and I will answer you, and will tell you great and hidden things which you have not known. Jeremiah 33:3 RSV

I had the verse printed on my prayer card with my photograph, the original of which my mother looked at that eventful night. God gave me many prayer partners, and one named Edith took on the task of prayer secretary, faithfully sending out letters for the next eighteen years. My prayer partners prayed faithfully, and when I came home on leave they welcomed me to their churches and homes, and in my link church at Nowra I'd spend a whole week visiting their out-lying centres also. My prayer partners everywhere were always keen to hear what God was doing in the places for which they prayed, and it was their work as much as mine.

People came to Berega church from far and near for the memorial service for the beloved Bishop Yohanna Omari, and Bishop Alfred Stanway took the service.

Raca had a bad habit of following me into church, just as he'd done with Enid, so, before the service, when I saw him amongst the crowd, I found a piece of rope and tied him to the bumper-bar of a car. He must have chewed through the rope, and when the Bishop was in the middle of the sermon, Raca walked up the centre aisle wagging his tail, and continued right to the front of the church and into the sanctuary. Bishop Stanway stopped speaking, and without comment stretched out his arm, pointing at the dog. He continued to point until one of the church elders came forward and shepherded Raca, whose tail had stopped wagging and was now between his legs, to return by the way he had come.

With the man walking behind him in silence, Raca walked back down the aisle. Growing more and more embarrassed, I fervently hoped he would pass by, but he saw me and turned in and curled up under my seat. The elder returned to his place, and the sermon continued.

"Just as a dog follows its master," said Bishop Stanway "in the same way Yohanna Omari followed his Master, and now he has gone to rest in his beloved Master's presence, for ever."

Chapter 13

"I'll be all right!" I told Enid when she went on leave, but I wasn't. I was terribly lonely, and unfairly I blamed the doctor's wife. "We should each make our own friends amongst the Africans," she had said when I first arrived. I had not made enough effort to do so and consequently I was now lonely, but I blamed Allison for being unfriendly.

I began to visit Paulo, the hospital chaplain, and his wife Aksa in the evenings. "*Karibu!*" Aksa would say when she'd finished cooking, "Welcome!" They taught me to eat *ugali*, a stiff pudding made of maize or millet, rolling some into a mouthful sized ball and dipping it into the *mchuzi* (usually red beans or vegetables)

After dinner I accompanied Paulo to the hospital where, by the light of a lantern he led in preaching, prayer and hymn singing. Eager for more, relatives and mobile patients accompanied us from ward to ward.

But I still felt lonely.

"Why don't you take Mapenzi home with you when you go off duty, Sister?" Staff-Nurse Mwendwa asked me one day. The five-months-old motherless baby had been left at the hospital to be cared for until she was big enough to eat solid food. She would lie in her cot and cry until a nurse picked her up and tied her on her back, where she rode happily while the nurse went about her duties. Following Mwendwa's suggestion, I asked the nurses to teach me to tie the baby on my back, and after that I often took her home with me at the end of the day. "*Papoo!*" she would say, lifting her arms to be picked up. It was her first word, meaning "Put me on your back!"

Next I had a cot brought down from the hospital, and kept her overnight when I was not on call. Sitting on the verandah with Mapenzi on my lap I watched the fireflies flitting about in the twilight, and greeted patients' relatives passing by on their way to the hospital. On my day off local children earned a few cents by minding her for me, and my mother sent toys for them to play with. Soon the sound of children's voices chased away the solitude. Mapenzi was changing my life, and I was changing hers. From a gaunt, miserable baby she was growing into a happy, chubby child.

*Jo with Mapenzi on her back, staff nurse Mwendwa
looks on approvingly, Tanganyika 1963*

But there were still times when I cried with loneliness. One day I read in my King James Bible: *Ye have compassed this mountain long enough: turn you northward Deuteronomy 2:3 AV*

A comment on this verse in a book by Amy Carmichael caused me to ask myself: *What is this mountain that you've been continually going round?*

It's a mountain of self pity, I confessed, seeing it for the first time, and I refuse to go round it any more. I'm tired of crying about it. I can't intrude on a married couple for company. I came out as a single person, and I must accept my singleness, and accept living alone. From now on I'll make my friends amongst the Africans.

It was my declaration of independence, and it would shape my life for years to come. I saw that resentment had been poisoning my life, but now it was gone. I confessed to Alison how I'd been feeling and asked her forgiveness, and she confessed to me that she too had been nursing resentment. She named some of the things I'd done which upset her and I apologised, and we forgave each other and prayed that God would forgive us and help us to change. It was a milestone in both our lives.

I'd often enjoyed Paulo and Aksa's hospitality but now I began to invite them over to *my* house. Just as we'd laughed as I learned to eat *ugali*, now there were peals of laughter as they practised using a knife and fork. Next I started a Swahili Bible Study in my home, and Paulo and Aksa, Mama Sala and all the nurses came. One night as we were singing a hymn, a nurse came in late with the mail. She handed me a letter, and while the others continued to sing, I read it:

"Dear Jo,

I am writing to tell you to finish at Berega at the end of this month and proceed to Murgwanza Hospital, where you will help Sister Faith Ward during the three months absence of Dr Rodda, who is going on study leave. When he returns, you should proceed to Kilimatinde Hospital, where you will be stationed from then on."

Yours prayerfully,
Alfred Tanganyika.

The letter came as a shock. I'd completely forgotten Bishop Stanway's words to me at two o'clock in the morning on Morogoro Station the night I'd arrived, almost two years before. *"You will be going first to Berega, and later to Murgwanza."*

"Berega - Murgwanza - Berega - Murgwanza" the train wheels had seemed to repeat as I tried to sleep, drumming the names into my memory lest I forget them. But I had forgotten all about Murgwanza, until now.

You've been going around this mountain long enough. Turn northward, the Bible reading that had helped me so much had said. The words had convicted me of my sin of self-pity, but now they had something more to say. *Turn northwards.* For me, northwards was the direction I must now take to the place to which I was going. Murgwanza was in the far north west of Tanganyika, on the borders of Rwanda and Burundi.

Mapenzi was big enough by now to survive at home, and her relatives would soon come for her. On my last day at Berega the river was up, preventing the doctor from taking me to the bus stand in his car. He came down to say goodbye, and as we shook hands he said solemnly, "If there is anything

I have said or done that has hurt you in the time you've been here, Jo, please forgive me."

"May I say the same to you, Ken," I reciprocated, and so we parted.

The nurses and Mama Sala accompanied me to the bus stand, the nurses carrying my luggage on their heads. Raca trotted beside us. When we got there Mama Sala prayed, and last goodbyes were said. As the bus started I waved out of the window and tears blew off my cheeks. Raca raced alongside until, winded, he dropped back.

It was the first of many sad partings which I would experience in the country that was already beginning to mean home for me.

Chapter 14

"Criminal Case Number 12" was due to be heard in Morogoro open court. I was the defendant, charged with allowing the hospital Land Rover to be driven in "an unroadworthy condition." A broken spring discovered by the police was seized upon as the cause of the accident. The unlawful licence of the driver was not mentioned. The spring could have broken at the time of the accident, but feeling it was my fault anyway, I followed the advice of the Indian lawyer and pleaded guilty, and once I'd paid the fine I was free to go.

My second year holidays were due. Months before, Genevieve, with whom I'd stayed at Mvumi, and Betty whom I'd replaced at Berega, had arranged for me to accompany them to Murgwanza for holidays. Now I was going there to work. We were travelling in Genevieve's car, and as soon as the court case was over we set out.

It was not the best time of the year for three women to drive halfway across Tanganyika in a small car, for the rainy season had started. After an overnight stop at the home of Swedish missionaries, we headed west, aiming to reach the isolated village where Genevieve's friends were stationed before nightfall. On one occasion we met a bulldozer clearing the mud so that a line of cars could get through. After that we didn't see another vehicle for miles. Genevieve began to teach us a chorus as we drove along:

Have you got any rivers you think are uncrossable?
Have you got any mountains you can't tunnel through?
God specialises in things thought impossible,
He can do just what no other can do.

As we were singing we came to an uncrossable river. The water was flowing swiftly, and the original bridge had been washed away. A new one had been partly built, with planks over which it would be possible to walk, but not to drive a car.

Through the curtain of falling rain we saw a car come to a stop on the opposite bank. "Well, I'm not going to just sit here." Genevieve declared in her usual practical manner. "I'm going over to talk to that other driver."

We sat and waited until Genevieve returned. The driver of the other car was a Swedish missionary on his way to pick up an important representative of their mission. Genevieve and he had agreed to exchange cars and meet three days later further up the river at Biharamulo where there was a bridge. Our new friend helped us to carry our loads across and install them in his car, then he carried his own gear over and waved to us from the window of Gen's little Volkswagen. We waved to him from the windows of his big new Swedish Volvo, and we all drove off.

After two days with our friends we drove into the yard of the Swedish Free Church at the appointed town, and Genevieve exclaimed in delight as she saw her own car standing there. The missionaries invited us in for afternoon tea and we told them about the song we'd been singing when we came to the uncrossable river. They knew it, and we all sang it together, they in Swedish and we in English, and then we prayed together and thanked God for getting us across the uncrossable river!

The sun was setting as we drove into Murgwanza. The hospital was built on the escarpment of the Rift Valley. Far below we could see the glint of a river, the boundary between Rwanda and Tanganyika. Years later the same river would run red with the blood of the Tutsi people in the genocide attempted by their Hutu neighbours.

Faith Ward, the Sister in Charge, welcomed us. It was two years since I'd wept and prayed in her sitting-room at Mvumi, when Swahili seemed impossible for me to learn. Now I was both understanding and speaking it! God had answered my prayers. Faith showed us around the hospital. The Maternity ward would be my responsibility, while she and the staff nurses looked after everything else. Dr Rodda had already gone on his study leave.

It was still dark when we went on duty in the mornings, and we huddled around a lantern while the night report was read. The whole area was wrapped in mist, and often it rained off and on all day. Clouds filled the valley. How different it was to sunny Ukaguru and Ugogo! The people here were different too, tall, and more reserved than the short, outgoing Wagogo and Wakaguru.

Patients who were too ill to walk were carried up the steep hills on home-made stretchers. Many suffered from multiple illnesses, including anaemia, caused by worms which bred in the damp soil and penetrated their bare feet. One young woman who was carried in on a stretcher seemed to be insane, and was grossly anaemic. As she lay helplessly in bed, unable to walk or even to speak, a large roundworm crawled up her throat and out of her mouth onto the pillow. She was riddled with roundworm, tapeworm and hookworm. In radio contact with Mvumi, Faith talked to Dr Joe Taylor.

Joe was a remarkable man. Many owed their sight to his skill in eye surgery, and others owed their lives to his skill in general surgery. As a boy Joe and his twin brother, with hundreds of other Jewish children, had been sent to England by their parents to escape Hitler's persecution. They never saw their parents again. Joe and his brother, with more than sixty other Czech children, were received into the Barbican Mission to Jews Children's Home. Both grew up to become committed Christians. Joe's brother ministered amongst the Jews in Israel, and Joe served the Lord as a missionary doctor. He worked at Mvumi hospital and as a flying surgeon with Christofel Blinden Mission, (*Christian Blind Mission*) training doctors in eye surgery in many African countries.

Joe was a fund of knowledge, and as soon as Faith described her patient's condition he remembered a rare type of tapeworm that can cause insanity. She was treated for tapeworm (and every other type of worm) and gradually her condition improved, and she recovered completely.

At the end of each day we took turns with an African staff nurse to be on call for the night. Hospital problems were the topic of conversation day and night, even at home. I began to feel as if I were never off duty, but when my day off came round there was nothing to do and nowhere to go. A persistent cough shook me, and in the cooler climate I couldn't throw it off.

Before coming to Murgwanza I'd read in my Bible, *I will plant them in this land in faithfulness, with all my heart and all my soul. Jeremiah 32:41b RSV* Even though I'd be at Murgwanza for only a few months, I wanted to be *"planted"* and to bear fruit. But now an insistent thought troubled me. *You're not being planted, you're being buried!* Satan, the one who insidiously plants negative thoughts in our minds, was at work in mine, but I didn't recognise it.

"Take a couple of days off," Faith advised. "Stay in bed." She found a pile of magazines for me to look through, amongst them an old copy of an English magazine, *Keswick Week.* In it I found an article on the story of Isaac and Rebecca.

Abraham had sent his servant back to the land of his birth to search for a bride for his son, Isaac. The first woman the servant met was Rebekah, daughter of Abraham's brother. She was a very suitable match for Isaac. The servant bowed his head and worshipped the Lord who had led him directly to the right girl. Bringing out gifts of gold and silver, he gave them to Rebekah. The girl took him home, where he explained his quest to her whole family.

And they called Rebekah, and said to her, "Will you go with this man?"

"I will go." she replied.   *Genesis 24:58 RSV*

"No one serves Christ for nothing," observed the writer. Just as the servant gave valuable gifts to Rebekah, so God gives precious gifts to those who follow his Son, and those who belong to Christ will inherit the kingdom of God.

"No one serves Christ for nothing." The words pierced my heart. I felt ashamed that God had needed to remind me of the many gifts he had bestowed upon me. Salvation, the Holy Spirit, eternal life .... the list went on and on. "Please forgive me for complaining, dear Lord," I prayed. Refreshed in body, mind and spirit, I returned to the hospital with renewed commitment.

Murgwanza hospital had no chaplain as Berega and Mvumi did, so it occurred to me that on my days off I could take the gramophone to the hospital and play gospel records to patients who would like to listen. Someone at home had given me a set of pictures illustrating the heart of man, and Sanzikora, an orphan boy at the hospital, went with me, helping to carry things. The little boy joyfully turned the handle of the gramophone, and in my broken but growing Swahili I dared to share the message of salvation through faith in Jesus.

My three months at Murgwanza came to an end. Dr Rodda was due back, and I said goodbye to Sanzikora and the patients and to Faith. Crossing Lake Victoria by ferry, I arrived at the guesthouse in Kampala, Uganda to spend two weeks of my overdue holiday. The hostess seated me at a small table by myself, and I felt lonely until I made friends with a motherly American woman named Edna Egemeier. She was from the Worldwide Grace Testimony Mission, and she gave me a small wall text on which were printed the words: *"Fear not, for I have redeemed thee." Isaiah 43:1*

The text was significant for Uganda at that time. The President, Idi Amin, was persecuting everyone who opposed him. Torture and killings were increasing, and our Anglican Archbishop, Janani Luwum, would be among those murdered by Idi Amin.

At the end of two weeks I re-crossed the lake by ferry and boarded a night train travelling south, and in the morning alighted at the small town of Manyoni. A jovial Welsh Church Army Captain, Gordon Johnson, met me at the train.

It was in Manyoni a few months later when I was driving the hospital Peugeot that I saw everyone in the street running. I got out and ran, too, and joined the outskirts of the crowd gathered around a police paddy-wagon. The people jostled me to the front, no doubt wanting to see the reaction of the *mzungu.* (white woman) I found myself a few centimetres from an enormous dead lion!

Its back was wedged along one side of the vehicle and its huge paws extended under the opposite seat. Its great stomach rose up in front of us, filled with the cow it had eaten just before it was killed ..... the reason the police had shot it. It had been raiding the villagers' cows. I stared at the great yellow canines a few inches from my bare arm, and thought, "What if it's not quite dead, and it opens its mouth to take one last bite?" Quickly I turned, and pushed out of the crowd.

At Kilimatinde a week later Gordon Johnson called out to me in passing, "Hey, Jo! You know that dead lion you saw in Manyoni the other day? The police in Dodoma measured it, and they said it was the second biggest lion ever shot in East Africa!"

But the day I arrived there were only a few monkeys to be seen playing in the baobab trees as Gordon drove me along the bush road leading to Kilimatinde, which, like Murgwanza was built on the ramparts of the Rift Valley. The thorn trees, the baobabs and the rising heat told me I was back in central region, and I felt as if I'd come home.

Chapter 15

The Rift Valley below shimmered in the haze as I sat on the rocks at "the point," gazing unseeingly into the distance, my mind intent on my own troubles. I was discovering that in each hospital where I worked I encountered new problems.

Full of enthusiasm, I'd gone into the ward which I'd been given and helped a nurse to sponge a patient. The African staff nurse felt threatened by my presence, and complained to the matron.

"Try to be in the ward as little as possible," said Joyce, who was both matron and tutor sister. "Let the staff nurses do rounds with the doctor by themselves, and you do your own round later. Just read what's written on the charts and make sure the treatment's being carried out." To the care of the linen room and drug store she added postal duties, to keep me busy.

Maybe it's God's punishment for complaining about too much work at Murgwanza, I thought erroneously. Now I have no patient contact at all! I tried to follow Joyce's instructions, but life seemed dull and unfulfilling after the hands-on ward work I'd participated in at Berega and Murgwanza.

"Why was I sent here? I'm superfluous! That's what I am, superfluous!" I grumbled. I didn't recognise the source of the bitter, negative thoughts that were attacking me. Satan was attacking me again.

Trying to be faithful in what I'd been given to do, late

one Friday afternoon I noticed that a child's blood count was dangerously low. A repeated test confirmed that he urgently needed a blood transfusion. I'm not superfluous after all, I thought happily, but although I now felt needed I still didn't feel wanted, and a root of bitterness remained. I didn't know how dangerous that was.

There seemed to be no niche into which I could fit to get to know the people, and so I sat by myself on my day off, gazing across the Rift Valley, but not really seeing it. Perhaps there's something I could do for God on my day off, I mused, something that no one else is doing. Closing my eyes, I prayed, "What can I do for *you*, dear Lord?"

I opened my eyes, and they focussed on a pale ribbon of road far below, running across the valley floor. Here and there along the road smoke was rising in the still air. There must be little villages down there, I mused. I wonder if they have churches, and I wonder if there are any Sunday schools? If not, perhaps I could go down on my day off and start some. The first thing to do is to ask the pastor.

"There are little churches in the valley" he replied, "but not even one Sunday school. You're welcome to go down and open some." He chose a Christian woman named Agnes to be the first teacher.

I obtained a diocesan Sunday School teaching manual and at daybreak the following Sunday wheeled my bicycle down the steep escarpment road. I needed to be there by 7am before the children went out to chase the birds and monkeys off their parents' crops. Children came running to meet me and to call Agnes. She came out with a big smile of welcome, and soon we were all in the little mud and sapling church, learning to sing Swahili choruses. A few weeks later she was ready to carry on alone.

Now I began to plan a second Sunday school at a village two miles along the road. In order to be there by 7am I needed to sleep in the first village. But Joyce objected strongly. "I can't allow you to sleep down there," she protested. " Something might happen to you, and I'd be responsible for letting you go."

I read in my Bible, *Fear not, ... have I not told you .... you are my witnesses! Is there a God besides me? Isaiah 44:8 RSV (abbrev)*

"If Bishop Stanway gives permission will you let me go?" I persisted. "Of course!" she agreed. "If he gives you permission he takes the responsibility."

Trips to Dodoma were few and far between, but Janet our doctor was away, and when a haemorrhaging patient needed urgent transfer to Dodoma hospital a few days later I went with her. She lay on a mattress in the back of the Peugeot and I sat beside her while Gordon drove, through pouring rain. The next morning at 9am I went to see the Bishop.

"Of course you can go down to the valley if you want to," he said when I told him why I had come. "That's what you came out here for! All missionaries are free to do what they want to on their days off. Just make sure you're back in time for duty. What are you doing for money?"

I admitted that I was using my own, and he wrote out a chit and handed to me. "Take that to the accountant," he said, "and he'll give you something for expenses."

The rain had gone, and driving home we found the world turning green and hundreds of frogs were jumping all over the road. My heart jumped with them, for joy! From then on, every Saturday afternoon I set out for the valley .

My trips enabled me to know something of the life of the people. Their long, flat-roofed dwellings were built of mud and sapling, and they had a minimum of furniture, all hand-made. At full moon, sounds of drumming and dancing could be heard as people made the most of the moon-light. If the rains failed there was famine, and men walked long distances looking for food. At such times women gathered grass-seeds to cook for something to give the children to eat.

Only twice was I ever afraid. In the middle of one night I woke up to find my heart thudding with fear. What had made me afraid, I wondered? Feeling for my torch, I flashed it around the floor, and seeing nothing I shone it through the branches of my thorn barricade. Outside, there was nothing to see but the stars shining peacefully down on the *pori* (grassland.) I'd been sleeping near the open doorway to get cool air, but now I moved further back inside. Committing myself into God's care, I went back to sleep.

In the morning Agnes asked, *Je, ulisikia kelele usiku?* "Did you hear the noise in the night?" "No," I replied. She told me that during the night a leopard had jumped over their thorn enclosure and carried off a goat. How thankful to God I was for waking me to warn me. I never slept near the open doorway again.

As I climbed the lonely escarpment one Sunday evening a drunken man came weaving his way down the road. As we drew level, he stopped. *Nataka kukuonja,* he said in a slurred voice, "I want to taste you!" Reaching out both my hands I placed them on his chest and gave an almighty push. He went staggering backwards down the slope, and at the same time I ran up it, shouting the Swahili help-cry which is like an Australian cooee. Once around the bend I scrambled up the embankment and hid in the bush. Slowly it grew dark, and when he did not appear I climbed down and hurried home.

When Joyce heard why I was late she enlisted the help of Dr Joe Taylor to try to dissuade me from going. "You're not very strong, you know. If you don't stop going down there I'll have you moved to Mvumi," he threatened.

I greatly respected Joe, but I knew I could never win an argument, so I kept quiet. Who was I to argue with the great Joe Taylor? But I had the great Alf Stanway's permission, and that, for me, was God's directive. Was not the Bishop over us all in the Lord, I reasoned?

"It's as if you only come alive when you go down there," Janet remarked wistfully. It was true. As soon as I started down the road, restrictions were left behind and I felt free. Love was flowing in the valley. By going down there I felt able to fulfil my missionary calling. The prophet Jeremiah best expressed how I felt when he wrote:

If I say, "I will not mention him, or speak any more in his name, there is in my heart as it were a burning fire shut up in my bones, and I am weary with holding it in, and I cannot." Jeremiah 20:9 RSV.

Joyce went home to England on leave and James our male nursing officer and I divided the matron's work between us. Heather, a young Irish sister joined the staff, and shared the sister's house with me. Janet went home to Ireland on leave, and Dr Bob Weedon from Australia took her place. One morning he drew my attention to a fluid balance chart that the nurses had not filled in. "If you weren't so exhausted from going down to the valley you would have noticed this," he observed.

His words hit home. On my previous safari, ten miles from Kilimatinde I'd felt overcome by the heat, and had lain down in the shade of a tree until I felt well enough to ride home. The hottest season before the rains had come. It was true that I'd not checked the chart, and true that I was very tired. I realised that the time had come to leave the Sunday schools to the African teachers.

I never went down to the valley again.

Chapter 16

I never went down to the valley again, but Bob did. He planned to start a Flying Doctor service to the Rift Valley with Kilimatinde hospital as its base. He arranged a trip in the hospital Peugeot to look for a suitable site for an airstrip. He was to go with our African Pastor, and they planned to leave at 6 am and to be away for three days. On the morning of the trip, a patient expecting twins came into labour. Bob waited until the twins were safely delivered, then said goodbye, but five minutes later I saw him staggering through the door carrying the inert form of a collapsed woman. Her relatives said she had fallen down a well. Bob's skilful examination revealed that she was suffering from a ruptured ectopic pregnancy, which had caused her to faint.

In the theatre Bob gave the anaesthetic while we prepared for operation and her relatives crowded around the window to see what we were doing to her. Suddenly her breathing stopped. "She's gone, Bob!" I exclaimed.

"No, by gum, she's not!" he responded. "You do mouth to mouth, while I stop the bleeding."

Hastily he gloved and gowned. At Bob's instruction a staff nurse removed the cap of a blood-taking bottle containing anti-coagulant and in it placed a sterile funnel lined with gauze to act as a filter. Swiftly opening her abdomen, Bob scooped up bowls full of blood, which he poured into the sterile bottle. The staff nurse hung up the unusual blood transfusion and ran it as fast as she could back into the woman's vein. Her own blood and Bob's daring and trust in God saved her life. Before long she was breathing for herself again, and as Bob was sewing up, she was waking up. The nurses transported her back to the ward and Bob said goodbye for the second time, then left to seek out a landing site for the plane.

It was 1966 and a time of political change had come to Tanganyika as President Nyerere's government embraced socialism. The people of the scattered rural population were encouraged to move into large *ujamaa* (family style) villages. This would facilitate the President's vision of providing water, school and a clinic for every village. The old system of chiefs and elders was being replaced by chairmen and ten-house chairmen, following the Chinese pattern.

I'd been at the hospital for almost two years, and my first home leave was due. Just before I left, a political meeting was held at which senior members of the hospital staff were criticised. Our nurses participated and as the meeting drew to a close and my name had not been mentioned I breathed a sigh of relief. "They're letting me off," I thought hopefully. But just before it ended I received a shock.

"And as for Sister Jo," said a staff nurse of whom I thought highly, "if she makes any more nurses cry, we'll report her to the Village Secretary!"

An incident where a rebuke of mine had perhaps been too sharp came to my mind, and I left Kilimatinde with a heavy heart. But on arrival in Dodoma there was something so interesting that momentarily I forgot the troubles I'd left behind. Genevieve, who was seconded to the SCF *(Save the Children Fund.)* doing child health surveys invited me to go with them on a safari. She would soon be leaving and it had been suggested that after home leave I might take her place.

On the sparsely grassed red earth the health workers,

Stanley and Alfred, set up green tents in the shade of a spreading thorn tree, being careful to avoid the path trampled down by elephants that sometimes drank at the nearby water-hole. The following day I helped to weigh malnourished babies in a canvas sling tied to the branch of a thorn tree, and to measure their frail biceps muscles. When we returned home that evening we brought with us several malnourished children and their mothers to the nutrition unit.

————•·•·•————

As the plane came in over Sydney a week later I watched a world I'd almost forgotten coming back into focus. Like someone in a dream I kissed my sister and her husband, then shook hands with the CMS representative. My mother was waiting at home. It was not until we walked outside that the cold winter air slapped my face and I knew that I was really home.

The air was even more bracing at Katoomba in the Blue Mountains where, after two happy weeks with my family, I attended a seminar at Hokonui, the ANCM holiday cottage. There, at two o'clock in the morning, I awoke in the ice cold mountain air and my mind became crystal clear. I lay awake, thinking.

Why had I caused the gentle brown eyes of a lovely staff nurse to fill with tears, and why had I made nurses cry? Far away from the situation, the Holy Spirit revealed to me the answer. I'd felt rejected by the staff nurse who hadn't

90

wanted me working in her ward. At Joyce's farewell the nurses had sung: "You're going away and leaving us with Sister Jeanne" The trainee nurses' love for their tutor sister was expressed in their song, together with their exuberant welcome to their new tutor.

A pang of jealousy had stabbed me. I'd tried to quell it by hardening my heart, but when I'd needed to rebuke a nurse for something, the hardness had been apparent.

In retrospect, I saw that it was natural for the nurses to be loyal to their tutors, who would help them to get through their exams and become qualified staff nurses, which was the ambition of every nurse. And it was natural for staff nurses to want to be in charge of their own wards without a white sister breathing down their necks. I had no need to feel either rejected or jealous. How sorry I was that I'd hurt that gentle staff nurse and others. I read in the Bible, *See to it that no one fail to obtain the grace of God; that no "root of bitterness" spring up and cause trouble, and by it the many become defiled; Hebrews 12:15 RSV.*

When I'd first gone to Kilimatinde and shared house with Janet and Joyce they'd explained to me how they tried to follow 1 John 1:7 as they shared house together, and they wanted me to do the same.

But if we walk in the light, as he is in the light, we have fellowship with one another, and the blood of Jesus his Son cleanses us from all sin.

It is impossible for human beings to live together and work together without sometimes causing offence. To "walk in the light" meant apologising when we caused hurt and telling others when they hurt us, so that the door could be open for reconciliation.

I tried to follow this now, writing to the staff nurse I'd

hurt, sharing with her what God had shown me, and asking forgiveness from her and the nurses. A letter came back sending me full and free forgiveness from them all.

Letters from Africa were to me now letters from home, and I eagerly scanned the first one that came from Joan, who had taken my place at Kilimatinde. She was sharing house with Heather, the Irish sister.

"A leopard crossed the path in front of Heather on her way back from the point the other day," she wrote, "and two lions came and roared back and forth to each other across our garden yesterday, from 4am till dawn."

As I read it I realised that from now on, as they walked up to the hospital at night, the two sisters might be wondering what might be in the bush by the side of the road! Scary stuff! How I thanked God that he had never let me either see or hear anything scary on my safaris.

After I went home I listened one day to a well known speaker who said that Christians should never make a move unless their whole team was in agreement. Did I, then, do the wrong thing by continuing to go to the valley in spite of opposition from our team?

I worried about it until one day I realised that I was forgetting something. Something that threw light on the whole thing.

Who had shown me the road so far below, as I sat at the point that day at Kilimatinde, asking God for something to do for him?

Who had gone with me down there?

Who had looked after me, bringing me safely home every time?

I believed it was the one who has promised when we

go out in his name, *"I am with you always, to the close of the age." Matt 28:20 RSV*

A letter from Jeanne, with whom I worked at Kilimatinde, had this to say:

"Yes, my friend, there were dangers at Kili. I was followed home from the hospital one night by a leopard. Our cat was walking beside me, and in the morning Earnesti, our house-boy, pointed out to me three sets of footprints ... mine, the cat's, and the leopard's.

But we were safe. Safe in the palm of his hand."

Chapter 17

"I think I've torn up my air ticket!

One of the first things I'd done on arrival home had been to clean out my wardrobe. There was junk from four years back, also my air ticket. That's finished with, I said, ripping up the ticket and adding it to the growing pile of rubbish.

When the first month with my family was over I "came down to earth" in an interview with CMS, in which I was given deputation assignments and a return date for Tanzania. Sitting in a taxi driving through the city afterwards I suddenly had a disturbing thought. I think my air ticket must have been a "return," and I think I tore it up!

I *couldn't* have torn up my air ticket, I argued in disbelief. When I got home I searched the wardrobe. There was no trace of it. My mother found me crying bitterly. "What's the matter with you?" she asked in astonishment. "I've torn up my air ticket and burnt it with the rubbish!" I sobbed. "When CMS find out they'll think I've gone mad and send me to a psychiatrist and I'll never get back to Tanzania!"

But God was not going to allow a torn up air ticket to prevent me from getting back to the place of his appointment.

"Jo! Have a bit of sense!" my mother admonished. "Don't you remember before we went away you wanted to burn the rubbish, and I said to you, "Don't go away and leave a smouldering incinerator. Put your rubbish in the garage until we get home.""

Hope revived. Running out to the garage, I brought in the large plastic bag full of old papers, and tipped them out on the floor. Amongst them were the pieces of my airline ticket. Fitting them together again, I sealed them with Sellotape, and when the time came, the ticket got me safely back to Tanzania.

A more disappointed person would have been difficult to find than I was on the day I arrived at Mvumi, and found that the sister who'd temporarily taken Genevieve's place on the SCF team (the job I'd expected to have) had fitted in so well she'd been asked to stay until the completion of the project. Instead of doing safari work, I was allocated to the children's ward.

You thought you loved children, didn't you, getting so excited about going on the safari team, I admonished myself. Weighing babies under a tree was one thing, but being responsible for a ward full sick children was another!

"I'm glad you've come to work in children's ward," said our Australian Matron as she showed me around the ward on my first day. "You'll be able to get these toilets cleaned up." We were inspecting the dingy toilet block as she spoke. As we continued around the ward she instructed me, "Mothers must not be allowed to take their children outside. Pathology staff complain to me that they can't find their patients."

Approaching the exit doors she gave a final warning: "In a week's time you should know all the children's names. The next time I come, I expect you to be able to tell me the name and diagnosis of every child when we do rounds." She walked briskly out the swing doors, her white uniform flashing in the sunlight, leaving me with a ward of fifty-six cots overflowing with eighty children. There were five trainee nurses to help me, plus the mothers. How I wished I had a staff nurse to help. "Jo, you're never satisfied," I scolded myself. At Kilimatinde you complained because the staff nurses didn't want you in their wards, and now you complain because you have too many patients and no staff nurse!

Many children suffered from multiple illnesses. Diagnosis charts often read: "Malaria; pneumonia; hookworm; anaemia; dysentery; dehydration." One day a child's chart read: "Tula malaka" meaning, literally, "eat the throat." It was the thing that had made me want to come to this country when I was fourteen years old. The baby's throat had been scratched and scraped with a specially grown long fingernail, and was terribly infected, just as Dr Paul White had described. I was amazed that twenty years later the cruel practice had not died out.

I'd been at Mvumi for a year when a letter arrived for me from the Bishop. Sister Lesley Bangham, a Church Army Sister from England at a small dispensary at Kalinzi, in the far west, would be due for leave in six weeks time. Would I go and relieve her? But he added, "You can accept or reject the appointment as you wish, because there is no doctor at Kalinzi."

Memories of times without a doctor at Berega came flooding back. Even a week without a doctor brought its problems. How would it be with no doctor at all for eight months? Others I could think of seemed to be far more suitable for the job. Barbara, for instance. She'd once withdrawn a bottle of her own blood (fortunately Group O) and transfused it into a patient, thus saving his life. That's the sort of person they ought to send to Kalinzi, I thought!

However, as Lesley was not going for another six weeks, and I was about to take three weeks holiday, I decided to wait to find out first whether or not this was God's appointment for me. Somehow, I believed, God would show me.

The sun had already set and the lights of the airport were coming on as the MAF plane landed at Nairobi airport. There being no night air traffic catered for at that time, the immigration officer had already gone home. "Don't forget to report to the immigration office in the morning to get your passport stamped," the pilot advised as we said goodbye. I completely forgot his words. After two weeks visiting friends in the Kingangop hills I returned to the Nairobi guesthouse, where I met my friend Patricia, and we discussed what we should do for the last week of our holidays. We decided to go to the YWCA in Mombasa, and took the night train, but once there we longed to get out of the city.

"The Children's Holiday Centre might take adults as it's not school holiday time," someone suggested. "Let's ring them, Tricia said enthusiastically." They had room for us, so we went to the market and bought a week's supply of food, including the biggest grapefruit we had ever seen. We then hired a taxi to take us to the Children's Holiday Resort. Dozens of beautiful palm trees, shaped by the prevailing winds, surrounded the cabins. We spent our days swimming and searching for shells in the blue-green water. Towards the end of our stay, the warden invited us to go to church with her at Mombasa Cathedral. The Dean was suffering from terminal cancer, she confided. The verse of Scripture he chose to speak on was 2 Corinthians 12:9

"My grace is sufficient for you, for my strength is made perfect in weakness."

I listened intently. This man was a living example of what he preached. In spite of cancer he was bravely carrying on his ministry, and as I listened to him the courage I needed came too. In the same promise in which the Dean was trusting, I also could trust. God's strength was sufficient for him in his weakness, and it would be sufficient for me in mine. I would accept Bishop Stanway's appointment and go to Kalinzi.

At four o'clock in the morning a few days later, a bus stood waiting for the last passenger at the border-post between Kenya and Tanzania. All passengers' passports had been checked except mine. "Why is he taking so long?" I wondered, as the immigration officer leafed through my passport again and again.

"I can't see where your passport was stamped when you came into Kenya," he finally exclaimed in a perplexed tone. Only then did I recall the pilot's words on the evening of my arrival: "Don't forget to go to the Immigration Office in the morning."

"It wasn't stamped," I admitted ruefully.

The officer's expression changed from perplexity to incredulous rage. "You've been an illegal immigrant in Kenya for three weeks!" he shouted. "I'm confiscating your passport. Go and take your luggage off the bus! You can return to Mombasa on the morning bus or you can go under police escort!"

"I'll go on the morning bus," I replied meekly, going to retrieve my luggage and tell Tricia what had happened. She would have stayed with me but she was expected at work on Monday morning. The bus roared off into the darkness leaving me standing on the road.

Returning to the immigration office I saw that the interview room door was now shut. The officer had evidently gone home to bed, and three policemen were sitting on stools at the counter, busily writing. There was no other seat. One of the policemen got off his stool and came over to me. "Come to my house." he said kindly. "My wife will give you a bed." Deeply touched, guessing that it might be her own or one of the children's beds, I thanked him but refused. "I'll sit outside on the grass," I said.

He was horrified. "You can't sit out there in the dark!" he protested. "A snake might bite you!" But I was adamant. The shock of seeing the bus go off without me had made it necessary for me to do the thing I always did when I was upset. I wanted to get alone and cry. Outside in the darkness, I found myself a private spot on the grass, and cried. When the growing light of dawn became strong enough to read by, I took out my small devotional book by Spurgeon, and at the page at which I prayerfully opened it I read:

For I was ashamed to ask the king for a band of soldiers and horsemen to protect us against the enemy on our way; since we had told the king, "The hand of our God is good upon all that seek him, and the power of his wrath is against all that forsake him." Ezra 8:22 RSV

Ezra had trusted God to keep him and his companions safe, with all the treasures of the temple which they were carrying, on their long journey home. God did so, commented Spurgeon, and the God of Ezra is our God today. My heart was comforted. God was with me, looking after me on my journey, just as he'd looked after Ezra on his.

The sun came up and a policeman came out and raised the flag. I took out the coffee and sandwiches I'd brought, and ate and drank. Just as I was finishing, I heard the sound of an engine, and looking up saw a car coming from Tanzania towards the border-post. The traveller and his wife were from India, I found. When they'd completed their passport check I politely inquired whether they could give me a lift to Mombasa. They could, and I got in.

Never had I travelled at such a speed, but suddenly we slowed to a halt. Some elephants were standing near the road, shielded by a few bushes. The man revved his engine repeatedly to frighten them and make them come out into the open, so that he could take a photograph. Gripping the back of the driver's seat, I watched breathlessly as the biggest elephant swung to face us, and began to sway ominously from side to side, flapping his enormous ears. Suddenly he lifted his trunk, and trumpeted loudly.

"Let 'er go, Mate!" I yelled at the driver. He and his wife burst out laughing. Whether or not he understood that in Australian idiom the car had suddenly become a horse and that he should let the horse "have its head," he got the message. The elephants were left unphotographed, and we took off like a rocket headed for Mars! I sat there chuckling at my broad Australian slang that had burst out, surprising even me.

Arriving in Mombasa, my kind helpers delivered me to the house of one of our missionaries. I was welcomed to stay the night, and the following day went to the Immigration Office. "Don't do it again!" the officer warned, handing back my passport, already stamped.

Once safely back at Mvumi, I got out my pad and pen. Trusting in the assurance of God's promise which I'd received at Mombassa, I wrote to Bishop Stanway and accepted his appointment to Kalinzi.

God's grace, I believed, would be sufficient for me in my weakness.

Chapter 18

A train lay on its side on the railway track, and a goods train stood waiting on the other side of the wreck. We walked past the derailed train to the goods train, and were given the choice of riding in a windowless van or an open truck. Other passengers chose the van, but I chose the truck. Standing behind the engine, the wind whipping in my hair, I revelled in the swiftly passing grasslands and the cloud-streaked sky, and sang at the top of my voice, the wind blowing it away. We were travelling through the region where the great missionary explorer, David Livingstone, had walked. Not far from Kigoma, I knew, was the place where the American reporter, Stanley, had found him, and greeted him with the now famous words, *"Dr Livingstone, I presume?"*

The train reached Kigoma, and Gordon Chittleborough, headmaster of the missionary Alliance Boys' School who had come to meet me, helped me down onto the platform. He carried my luggage to his car and drove me to his home, where his wife Marion had a welcome lunch ready. After we'd finished eating Gordon took me out onto the verandah and pointed to a line of blue hills above the town. "Kalinzi's up there," he said. "There's an old Peugeot pickup with a canvas covered back that you can use to carry patients in if you want it. Lesley doesn't drive. She sends a man on a bicycle to the Seventh Day Adventist Hospital thirty miles the other way at Manyovu when she needs a doctor."

I considered the matter. If I drove thirty miles and found the doctor away it would mean I'd wasted sixty miles, as I'd have to come back and then drive down to Kigoma Government Hospital. And with the Peugeot I'd get down to see Gordon and Marion when I had to bring a patient in. I thanked Gordon and accepted it, and he promised to get it repaired and bring it up to me.

The next morning Gordon drove me up the steep road to Kalinzi. Would I have the courage to drive on that narrow, winding road in the wet season, I wondered? Only four-wheel drive vehicles could use the road once the rains came, Gordon reassured me. From the highest point in Kalinzi the faint outline of mountains in the Congo could be seen far across Lake Tanganyika in the west, and in a northerly direction were the rolling hills of Burundi.

On arrival, Lesley took us on a tour of the hospital. There was a room for outpatients, a labour ward, a small ward for men and one for women, plus staff houses. All had been built under Lesley's directions ten years before. Sixty-three years old, with piercingly blue eyes and iron-grey hair drawn back in a bun, barely five feet tall and no light weight, Lesley was a woman to be reckoned with. When she shouted for a nurse her voice could be heard all over the establishment!

I met the nurses, all of whom Lesley had trained. The oldest was Emily, who had one day walked too close to an animal trap, not realising that a leopard had been caught in it. It had sprung on her, clawing her face and scalp. Relatives carried her up the hills to Lesley, who stitched her wounds and nursed her back to health. She stayed on to become a Christian and a faithful hospital worker.

Habeli, Lesley's house-help, was an older man whom Lesley had brought with her from Berega, together with his wife, Beatrice. In those ten years Lesley had delivered all of their six children, as well as the children of villagers for miles around. In addition to midwifery she treated up to one hundred and twenty out-patients a day. Amongst them were dental cases. Never having been taught the art of injecting into the gums, she worked without local anaesthetic. One morning before she left a pregnant woman came for tooth extraction, and Lesley offered to demonstrate her technique for me.

Seating the woman on a low box, she first prayed aloud, then, grasping the tooth firmly in her forceps, she rocked it to loosen it. The woman gave a low groan, and I suddenly felt faint. Turning, I fled, not stopping until I reached the house and lay down. "Whatever happened to you?" Lesley asked when she came over for lunch. I apologised, and made a mental note that, having been shown before leaving Australia where to inject local anaesthetic, I would use it! But I decided not to pray aloud. The patients might see how inexperienced and scared I was if I prayed aloud, I thought. I would pray for God's help, silently, in my heart.

After Lesley had gone, the dentistry went well until a tooth refused to come out. All my rocking and tugging achieved nothing, and finally there was only one thing to do. "Would you like us to pray?" I asked the patient. *Ndio!* He agreed quickly. "Yes!" So I prayed aloud, asking God's help, and to our astonishment the tooth just lifted out like taking a piece of cake. After that I always prayed aloud!

A young mother asked permission to wait at the hospital for the birth of her baby. Two weeks passed, then one evening she came into labour. At midnight I returned to the house to make a lime drink, then went back to labour ward. At 2am the baby was born. When it was all over I walked back to my house carrying the brightly flaring pressure lamp. Coming up the steps of the verandah I saw that my bedroom door was wide open. Had I forgotten to close it when I came over at midnight? Holding the lamp aloft, I peered inside. Everything had been thrown around in disarray, and Lesley's trunk was missing. I fled back down the steps and ran to the nurses' quarters, for Habeli was away on holidays. *Amka, Amka!* "Wake up, wake up!" I yelled to the nurses. *Wezi!* "Thieves!"

We ran to the church pastors, and they came back with us. The wooden door to the hospital safe had been smashed, but they'd been unable to open the inner iron door. A key that fitted my bedroom door had been dropped beside my bed, and a *panga* (large knife) had been dropped in the middle room.

Suddenly we heard heavy, running footsteps outside, and gave chase. In the garden our two hospital bicycles had been discarded, and one of the pastors mounted one and I the other. With the hissing pressure lamp still in my hand, we gave chase. There was no sign of them, and at last we stopped. The pastors stood at the edge of the hilltop, and shouted into the darkness, *Ooo-eee! Ooo-eee! Sista ameibiwa!* "Help! Help! Sister's been robbed!" Within minutes we were joined by a dozen men carrying clubs and spears. They didn't find the thieves, but they found everything that had been stolen, and carried them home again, including Lesley's belongings and a basin of eggs left standing on the road. Not one egg was broken! I thanked God for his perfect timing of the young mother's labour, which had taken me out of the house when the thieves came.

A woman expecting twins did not accept my advice to go down to the Government hospital to await the birth of her babies. The first I delivered normally at midnight, but after that she went out of labour. The following day I first treated the outpatients and then drove her down to Kigoma hospital, and went to Gordon and Marion's to spend the night. The next morning I called at the hospital to see how she had got on.

Alifariki, said the nurse. "She died."

"What? Whatever happened?" I asked, aghast. The nurse explained that the doctor had decided to do a Caesarean. He had given the mother a spinal anaesthetic, and she immediately collapsed and died, before they could operate. The spinal anaesthetic had not suited her, no doubt due to her advanced labour. Deeply sad, Habeli and I drove home. Suddenly I felt very tired. Emergency had followed emergency, and I longed for a rest.

Not long afterwards, while driving a dehydrated baby to Kigoma hospital, there seemed to be no power in the engine. Going downhill we gathered speed, but on the up-grade the engine chugged more and more slowly, only just managing to get over the top. Finally, ten miles out of Kigoma it gave up altogether.

We sat there for two hours until a truck came along. Opening the bonnet, the driver and his companion leaned over and peered into the mysteries of the interior, but failed to find the problem. He offered to drive us to Kigoma. We climbed in, leaving Habeli to mind the Peugeot. Mother and baby safely admitted to hospital, I walked to the school where I knocked on Gordon and Marion's door. They warmly welcomed me as usual, and the following morning Gordon and a mechanic drove me out to where faithful Habeli was minding the Peugeot. As the mechanic's examination progressed, Gordon asked me, "When did you last put oil in the engine?"

"Two days ago" I replied, truthfully.

"Well, the mechanic says there's none in it now," he

said. "Always check the oil just before driving it. If you'd driven one more mile without oil the engine would have been ruined."

He probably doesn't believe that I put oil in it, I thought, but I knew that I had. What had happened to the oil? On further examination a broken gasket was discovered. I didn't know what that was, but Gordon explained that the oil was mixed in with the water. The thing that had stopped the car was a different problem altogether, one easily fixed. New points were needed, and had been in the Peugeot's tool box all the time! How I thanked God that the car had stopped just in time to save the engine. I felt comforted that God was watching over me, the patients, and the Peugeot!

Early the next morning we were on our way again. Not far out of Kigoma an old man hailed us. Feeling sorry for him, I stopped, and since he too was going to Kalinzi, I told him to get in. But when I tried to start the engine again, it refused to kick over. Once more we sat waiting, hoping for help to come along. I began to feel angry, and to understand Lesley's wisdom in refusing to have a vehicle. At last a truck came along, and the driver stopped and opened up our bonnet. The mysteries of the interior were again explored. There was only one thing to do, he said – remove our self-starter! "Go ahead and do it," I agreed. He did so, and then gave us a push-start. The engine fired, and we were off, with shouted instructions from our helper not to stop until we reached Kalinzi. We didn't!

Three months went by, then one day Gordon arrived with the mechanic who fixed the self-starter, checked everything, and they left. The following day I saw a crowd coming, carrying a woman on a home-made stretcher. It was the first emergency in three months. On examination in the labour ward, I found her to be in an advanced state of obstructed labour. The men lifted her onto a mattress in the back of the Peugeot and I drove her down to Kigoma Hospital, but in spite of our getting her there safely, she died three days later.

That was my last trip to Kigoma. The wet season had come, and the roads became impassable except for four-wheel drive vehicles. After that, as Lesley had done, I sent a man by bicycle to Manyovu when I needed a doctor. He came, a cheerful young American, and took our patients to his hospital.

One windy, black night of torrential rain, two patients at one time needed urgent medical help. At two o'clock in the morning, above the deafening roar of rain on the roof, I was relieved to hear the sound of the doctor's Land Rover. He examined our patients and agreed that each needed a Caesarean, but one patient refused to go. Without her husband's permission she was afraid to leave, and the doctor had to go without her. She laboured on for two more days, and finally delivered a dead baby. I thanked God that the mother survived.

After eight months away Lesley returned, and I said goodbye to all with whom I'd worked. I would never forget Kalinzi. Before going there I'd placed my trust in God's promise: *"My grace is sufficient for you, for my power is made perfect in weakness." 2 Corinthians 12:9 RSV*

God had kept his promise.

Chapter 19

Despite all we could do, children were dying. One chubby boy three or four years of age had both legs strung up in plaster. Another child who was put in his cot with him subsequently developed measles, and the little boy in plaster caught it and died. Two sisters aged nine and eleven were in for malaria and were better and going home. On the morning of discharge both had elevated temperatures again. They developed measles, and slowly their condition deteriorated until they lapsed into coma. We tube fed them, and when we cleaned their nostrils, no matter how gently, pieces of mucus membrane sloughed off. The same was happening in their mouths and inside their eyelids. After a long struggle to save them, both sisters died.

Babies suffering from measles lay semi-conscious, their sunken eyes half open. To save their corneas from drying out we taped their eyelids shut to prevent the blindness that results from corneal ulceration. One afternoon I found our African doctor in tears. "The father of that baby boy who just died blames me for his death, Sister," he said sadly. "What more can I do than I'm doing?"

"If only we had anti-measles vaccine!" I sighed. "If all these children had been vaccinated against measles they might not have died!"

"Yes," agreed one of our missionary doctors, "but we can't vaccinate all the children in Ugogo, and we don't have the money for anti-measles vaccine." I prayed that God would somehow provide the needed vaccine.

Pressures in the ward were matched by stresses at home, where three nursing sisters shared one house. One day after an unhappy incident I moved into an empty flat at the end of the building. The sister with whom I'd had words made a cake and left it on a table in my flat when I was out.

"Does she think a cake can make up for the way she hurt my feelings?" I thought angrily. Picking up the plate with the cake on it I took it back and left it in her kitchen.

And now something terrible happened. The words of the Bible which had always spoken comfort to me now only convicted me of my sin. Jesus warned, *"but if you do not forgive men their trespasses, neither will your Father forgive your trespasses." Matthew 6:14* RSV

Every day I went on duty with a heavy heart. When news spread like wildfire that a herd of elephants was walking past the hospital everyone who could leave their wards, staff and patients alike, ran up the hill to see them. Everyone except me. I felt too unhappy to care about anything, even a herd of elephants walking past Mvumi hospital!

At last the realisation came that to have peace with God I must make peace with my fellow sister. Going to her, I apologised and asked her forgiveness. God's word again spoke forgiveness and comfort to me, and all was well. Elephants may never forget, but humans have to! Otherwise we forfeit God's forgiveness for ourselves, Jesus warned.

Having moved to the flat I now had to live with what I'd done, and I felt terribly lonely. Remembering how God had taught me to cope with loneliness before, I followed the same pattern. Dan, a sixteen-year-old boy from the village often dropped in for a talk, and I suggested we go to start Sunday Schools in two small villages that had none. On my day off we set out, and in the weeks that followed Dan was able to carry on alone. Later he did a three months course at the Bible School at Msalato, then a nine months course, and long after I'd left Mvumi I heard that Dan had become a pastor.

Unexpectedly a letter came from the Bishop. I was to go immediately to Berega to relieve the sister, Jean, who was going to England to do a midwifery tutor course. The prospect of returning to my first hospital filled me with delight. As the train travelled east I gazed nostalgically out at the yellow grassed plains of Ugogo passing by and the blue hills of Ukaguru coming closer. Returning to my seat, I took out my Bible and Scripture Union notes. The reading for the day was Genesis 13.

So Abram went up from Egypt .....And he journeyed on from the Negeb as far as Bethel, to the place where his tent had been at the beginning....to the place where he had made an altar at the first; and there Abram called on the name of the Lord. Genesis 13:1-4 RSV

How apt the words were for me, travelling back to the place where I'd first worked when I came to this country. As I meditated on it I remembered that I'd once prayed to go around the villages with Paulo the evangelist, preaching the gospel on my day off, but it had not been meant to be. Now I saw that my prayer had been answered in a different way. God had taken me north, south and west, to Murgwanza, Kilimatinde, Mvumi and Kalinzi, and in every place I'd had the opportunity to scatter some seeds of the gospel. And now God was taking me east again.

At Berega the river was up, so the nurses met me at the bus-stop. Lifting my luggage onto their shoulders, they led me along the same path by which I'd walked out seven years before. Suddenly I saw Raca in the distance, and he saw me. He began to race in circles, wild with excitement. His ecstatic circling brought him to my feet, where he jumped all over me, yelping with delight, while I patted him, amazed that he still remembered me. When his excitement abated, he led us, tail wagging, to the sisters' house. Jean came out, followed by Alma, the German sister, carrying a baby under each arm. "Meet the orphans! We have ten! " she said happily as we went inside." At night I'll look after nine, and I'm giving you one." With that, she deposited a chubby nine-months-old baby boy on my lap. "This is Musa."

How would I manage to look after the hospital and a baby too, I wondered, forgetting that the last time I'd been here I had Mapenzi to look after when I came off duty. In church that Sunday the sermon was on the verse that had helped me so much before: *"My grace is sufficient for you for my power is made perfect in weakness.*

Wendy, a Mothers' Union worker came to share house with me, as Enid had done. Alma and the orphans lived up one end of the house and we lived down the other. There was a cot in my room for Musa, and he came crawling to me whenever he saw me. Wendy and I both enjoyed helping Alma with bottle-feeding the orphans in the evenings. In the middle of one night I'd just fed Musa when I was called to the hospital. Hearing him crying and seeing my bed empty, Wendy made him a bottle. In the morning two empty bottles told us that Musa had drunk two feeds and had gone happily back to sleep with no ill effects.

The years I'd been away had seen many changes. Dr Robert Gurney had replaced Dr Ken Dalley and an African Medical Assistant now joined the team. Mariamu the nurse-aide had completed her schooling and had done general training at Mvumi. She'd spent a post-graduate year in Dar-es-Salaam where she qualified as an A-grade sister, and after I left she would become the hospital's first African matron.

My eighteen months at Berega had many trials, but a few years later when I came back for a visit I found two of the nurse aides were now qualified staff nurses. They had done their training at Kilimatinde, and they proudly showed me around the hospital.

God has not promised us life without pain, but Jesus has promised to be with us, and therefore in spite of our trials, mistakes and tears, our work will not be in vain.

While I was at Kalinzi a letter from my mother had told me she'd had a breast removed for cancer. A letter from her doctor now said that the cancer had spread to her spine, and she was undergoing deep x-ray therapy. As I walked Berega's bush road that evening I wept, and pleaded with the Lord to heal her. My leave and home service was almost due, and for the months I'd be home I wanted us to be together. But she'd sold the house and had moved into a retirement village near our church, St Anne's, at Ryde. There would not be enough room for me to stay with her.

As I prayed about it, the thought came to write to the Rev John Reid at Christ Church in Gladesville, which had been our church when I first came to know the Lord. Someone there might have a flat or a house, I thought, that we could rent for the eight months I'd be home. But as the plane took off for Australia there had been no reply, and I was conscious of the fact that for the first time in my life I didn't have a home.

Chapter 20

At Mascot Airport in Sydney a CMS representative waited until my family and I had exchanged greetings, then he too welcomed me warmly and handed me an envelope. Eagerly I tore it open, and found it was from John Reid. He had in his parish a lady named Mrs Paton who had offered the use of her house to my mother and me for my leave and home service. She was away caring for her sick elderly sister.

As on my first leave, my aunt Marj gave me her car to use. She had already bought another to replace it, and would sell the old one after I'd gone back. We drove over to see Mrs Paton's cottage. There was a bedroom for my mother and a sun-room for me to sleep in. I'd be able to sit up in bed at night and watch the car lights coming across Gladesville bridge – a beautiful sight to someone just back from four years in the bush! Linen, blankets, crockery and cutlery were all provided, and there was a lock-up garage for the car. My mother and I remembered Jesus' promise, *"every one who has left houses or brothers or sisters or father or mother or children or lands, for my name's sake, will receive a hundred-fold, and inherit eternal life." Matthew 19:29 RSV.*

The vineyards had been sold, and we went to stay with the family, Keith, Kath and Marj, in their lake cottage at Sunshine. While we were there, plans were made for my mother to move to a larger unit at Hopetoun Village in Castle Hill. While home I'd be able to help with the move. In spite of her fight with cancer my mother was her usual sparkling self, and once more she became my companion and navigator as I drove to speaking engagements. There were new contacts to make and those who had prayed and supported the work to be visited, and we especially enjoyed our drive down the beautiful south coast to Nowra, where we stayed for a week with hospitable CMS supporters. We also renewed friendships at Gerringong, Berry, Huskisson and Bomaderry.

During my last few weeks at home every plane that flew over reminded me that soon I'd be leaving my mother again. Would she still be here when I returned in four years time, I wondered? But it was not the thought of leaving my mother that made the tears flow as I knelt in the front row of the packed auditorium at Katoomba Conference Centre for our farewell service. A letter just handed to me had broken the news that on return I was to report to Mvumi Hospital. I was glad no one behind me could see my tears, but from those who administered the bread and the wine there was nowhere to hide. The tears just flowed down my cheeks and wouldn't stop.

One of those serving us was Bishop Stanway, home from Tanzania. After the Service I pushed through the crowd to say goodbye, and taking my hand in his big, warm handshake, he commented meaningfully, "Jo, *the blessing of the Lord makes rich, and he adds no sorrow with it.*"

I looked up the verse of Scripture when I got home and found it was Proverbs 10:22, but I found it difficult to understand. That God's blessing is our greatest wealth I understood, but that he adds no sorrow with it I found hard to comprehend. Had not my times at Mvumi caused me much sorrow; and was I not going back to sorrow again? I'd always found being in charge of a ward difficult, but the busy children's ward at Mvumi I'd found almost impossible to cope with. And living with others whose age and interests were different to mine also had its problems.

My sister and niece drove me to the airport, and the moment of final good-byes came. As I followed the crowd through the barrier and up the steps of the aircraft I felt alone again, but as the bump of the jet's wheels folding into place told me we were airborne, peace filled my heart as I remembered again Jesus' promise, *"I am with you always, to the close of the age." Matthew 28:20 RSV*

At Mvumi our previous superintendent, Dr Joe Taylor and his wife Joan had left. Joe was now specialising, flying all over Africa to teach eye surgery. An Australian doctor, Peter Bolliger and his wife Robyn had come to take Joe and Joan's place. Both welcomed me warmly. Not yet knowing where I was to live or work, I walked up to the house where I'd previously lived to greet the sisters, and we had a cup of tea together.

While we were catching up on news the new African Matron, Milika Kongola, walked up the path. She greeted me with a warm smile, then joined us for tea. As we sat talking she said, "Jo, since the SCF team finished its project and left we've had no funding for safari work, and we've only had Stanley and Alfred to go out to the villages to do a little health teaching. At the Nutrition Unit there's just Mama Aksa the house-mother, and sometimes we've only had one or two mothers and babies in the rooms. We feel that what is needed to give the work a boost is to have a sister there again, and we thought of you. Would you like to do it, Jo?"

Would I like to do it? It was the work I'd so looked forward to doing when I returned from leave last time, and my disappointment had been profound when I wasn't able to join the team. And now Milika was asking me – would I like to do it?

"I'd love to do it!" I exclaimed, jumping up and giving her a hug. "Thank you Milika!"

'"There are two new staff houses being built just down the road from the old mission house," she continued. "We've decided to give one to you."

It all sounded too good to be true. I remembered Bishop Stanway's verse of Scripture: *"The blessing of the Lord makes rich, and he adds no sorrow with it."* Now only one thing remained to make my joy complete. "Dear Lord," I prayed, "I don't want to live alone. Please, please give me someone to share the house!" A few weeks later Janet, the doctor with whom I'd so happily shared house at Kilimatinde returned from leave, and was appointed to Mvumi. She accepted Milika's invitation to share the new house with me. God had indeed given his blessing, and had added no sorrow with it.

Theo Kitchen, the doctor in charge of the project, called a team meeting in his house, and his wife Liz welcomed Mama Aksa the nutrition house-mother, Stanley and Alfred the two health workers, and me. "The Dodoma Council have promised us a small grant of money to recommence safari work," Theo told us, and they'll supply a Land Rover and a government driver. It will mean the nutrition team can get out on safari for a few days each week. I'd like to hear your ideas on what kind of work we should do."

There was silence for a while, each busy with their own thoughts. My mind went to the mothers and babies who had come too late to save their lives when I first came out, and compared that with the many healthy mothers and babies now attending our clinics.

"I think we should start baby clinics in the villages," I proposed. "We could do ante-natal checks too. We could bring women here and give them a week's training in child care, and they could be our helpers when we go to their village."

Everyone agreed, and together we worked out a plan. We would sleep out in the villages three days a week for the first three weeks of each month, educating the village chairmen and all the people about what a baby clinic was. During the last week of each month we would train women chosen by the their own villages, and they would be our helpers when we came.

As I stood in the drugstore in the early mornings preparing safari vaccination kits that included anti-measles vaccine, I thought of the children who had died during the measles epidemic and I thanked God for answering our prayers and supplying the much needed vaccine, and a way to get it out to the villages. Soon under-nourished children filled the Nutrition Unit, and the mothers learnt to make nutritious foods. Emaciated babies gained weight and went home, and during the next five months we opened twelve mobile clinics.

In the evenings I visited Mama Aksa and the mothers, and we sat around the dying embers of their cooking fires as Aksa told Bible stories in their tribal language, Cigogo, and led Cigogo prayers and hymn singing. When Aksa retired a younger woman, Foibe, took her place.

When we commenced our work there were no canvas safari beds available in Dodoma, so I bought an iron folding stretcher. It had one problem – the iron links that formed the mattress had a habit of falling out as the Land Rover jolted over the rough terrain. One evening on return from safari there were only two links left attached to the frame. Tired and impatient, I removed the last two links and threw all of them into a box. I carried it into the house and dumped it down, declaring I'd never again re-connect it. "That's the end!" I stormed. "I'll never use that thing again!

But inevitably the time came for the next safari. What would I sleep on? Tears of frustration flowed. How could I ever connect it all up again? I felt the task to be beyond me. Suddenly there was a call of *Hodi!* at the door ....the Swahili equivalent to a knock. *Karibu!* "Come in!" Janet and I shouted. It was Robbie Carmichael, the young English doctor who lived opposite. "What's the matter, Jo?" he asked, noticing my red eyes, "Anything I can do?"

I showed him the links of my broken bed. "Every time I hook those links onto the frame they fall out again!" I declared hopelessly. "I just give up!"

"Back in a tick!" said Robbie, disappearing in the direction of his house. Within minutes he was back, sitting down on our circular grass mat, reconstructing my safari-bed. With his pliers he carefully tightened every link as he hooked them onto the frame and on to each other. It was like putting together a jigsaw puzzle. Those links never fell out again.

It was an act of kind and humble service that Robbie did for me that day, and as I sat watching him do it, his kindness made up for much of the loneliness I'd experienced at Mvumi. I'd been the odd one out, with different interests to others. I'd pursued my own path, but here was a young doctor who cared sufficiently to sit on the floor reconstructing my safari-bed. Robbie didn't know it, but I felt that his kindness was reconstructing not only my safari-bed, but helping to reconstruct my life at Mvumi.

Had I not returned to Mvumi I would always have remembered it with sorrow, but now I would always remember it with joy. It was the place where God gave his blessing and added no sorrow with it.

Chapter 21

I crouched on the floor, vomiting into the bowl of the toilet. It seemed suffocatingly hot. I'd woken feeling sick and suffering from diarrhoea, and my first thought was, Oh, no! I won't be able to go on safari!

I felt terrible. Perhaps tomorrow I'll be better and able to go, I thought. But when I caught sight of my reflection in the mirror I stared aghast at the image that looked back at me. The eyes were yellow. "Oh, no!" I groaned again. "I'm jaundiced!"

It was as I guessed – infective hepatitis. A staff-nurse was allocated to my job, and for three weeks Janet nursed me while the jaundice slowly faded. I became so bored that I walked around on my bed squashing mosquitoes on the ceiling. In the fourth week an unexpected invitation came from the doctor and his wife at the Hombolo Leprosy Centre, Guy and Dawn Timmis, to stay with them for a week to convalesce.

Most of the week was spent sitting on the lawn enjoying Dawn's beautiful garden, and laughing at Guy's wit, but as each day passed I looked forward more and more to returning to Mvumi and getting back to work. On my last evening, the centre's nursing sister, Barbara Young, invited me to her house for dinner.

"I have something to share with you," she confided, displaying a sparkling ring on the third finger of her left hand. "Ian and I are engaged." Her fiance was a fellow missionary - a teacher at the diocese's high school in Dodoma.

"I don't know who the Bishop has in mind to take my place," she said after I'd congratulated her, "but whoever it is, I hope they'll take Pooch and Psyche. They might get run over in the town." Pooch was a big blond cat and Psyche a small Maltese terrier that originally had belonged to Corrie, the sister at Dodoma's psychiatric hospital.

"Whoever it is will have to come here soon," Barbara continued, "so that they can learn about the place before Guy goes on furlough. Its only six weeks until he goes, and he's not very happy that I won't be here. He's been training me to take his place."

"Well, there's one thing certain," I replied, "it won't be me! I don't know a thing about leprosy, and I've only been doing the mobile baby clinics for five months. The Bishop's not likely to move me so soon."

"How can you be so sure?" asked Barbara.

"The mobile clinics are a new project. We're just getting them established, and it's work I love more than anything I've ever done!" I explained. "And anyway, God knows that I don't have the right gifts for this sort of work." I'd once seen Win Preston, Hombolo's previous sister, sitting outside the Bishop's office, waiting to see him. "Another *shauri*" she'd said wearily, explaining that patients sometimes lived in the leprosy centre for years, and consequently had many *shauris* (problems) I'm glad I don't work there, I'd thought.

"Besides all that," I went on, God knows that I *can't sew!*" The centre had a sewing room where working patients machine-mended patients' clothing and hospital linen, and I imagined that if anything went wrong with a machine the sister would have to sort it out.

But I'd forgotten something – a sermon that had helped me before coming out, when I'd been in a panic over this very thing, my lack of sewing expertise. The Rev Reg Langshaw at St Anne's Ryde had preached on Isaiah 33:21.

All the capital cities of the ancient world were built on rivers, he said, but Jerusalem, God's chosen city, had no river. Isaiah the prophet wrote: *But there the Lord in majesty will be for us a place of broad rivers and streams. Isaiah 33:21 RSV*

"God himself would make up the deficiency," Reg said. "And when we set out to serve God, God will make up for our deficiencies, too."

It was great to arrive back at Mvumi. Janet was home, but about to go up to the hospital. "It's lovely to see you looking well again," she said warmly. "There's a letter for you on the table beside your bed." She hurried off, and I took my bag to my room, looking curiously at the letter propped up against my lamp. I could tell by the crest stamped upon it that it was from the Bishop. Tearing it open, I began to read.

Dear Jo,

Barbara Young is engaged to be married, and you are to proceed to Hombolo Leprosy Centre to take her place.

Dr Timmis is going on leave in six weeks time, and I understand that he is about to attend a leprosy seminar. I have suggested that you accompany him to the seminar to brush up on your knowledge of leprosy, as you will be in charge of the Leprosy Centre during his absence. I will be praying for you in your new appointment, which will take place as from now.

Yours sincerely in Christ, Alfred, Tanganyika.

I knelt down beside the bed and cried tears of shock and disappointment, but even as I pleaded with God to reverse the Bishop's decision, the truth slowly dawned. It was not just the Bishop's decision, it was God's appointment.

Hurriedly I packed. My luggage was to be transferred to Hombolo while I was at the seminar, and by Monday morning my green tin trunk and suitcases stood ready in the room that had been mine, but which now was stripped of identity. Guy Timmis's car drew up at the door, and as I said goodbye to Janet and a mental goodbye to everyone at Mvumi, the sun rose behind the baobabs and the scene imprinted itself on my memory. Early as it was, Stanley was there to see me off, and he led us in prayer. We committed each other to the care of our heavenly Father.

Kwa heri, dada yangu! "Goodbye, my sister! "

Kwa heri, ndugu yangu! "Goodbye, my brother!"

With Stanley's double handshake and a hug from Janet, I got into the car and was driven away.

Knowing nothing about leprosy, I found the seminar intensely interesting. I'd thought when I left the clinics that my days of health teaching, which I loved, were over, but now a whole new field of health education emerged. I learnt that by teaching people who had lost all feeling in their hands such simple measures as the use of pot holders, it was possible to prevent the loss of fingers through constant burns, and there were many more such simple measures to teach. When we returned to Hombolo, my education continued with Guy's lessons in diagnosing and treating leprosy.

Barbara had left me Pooch, her cat, and also her dog, Psyche, and the Timmises had asked me to mind their dog while they were away. My friends Theo and Yvonne in Dodoma now asked me to take their cat too, because they were going home for good. I said, "I'm sorry, but it's impossible. I already have two dogs and a cat to look after!"

"Do you know what Stephen (their younger son) said in his prayers last night?" Yvonne asked me the next time I came to I stay. "He said, `Lord Jesus, please make Aunty Jo want to take our cat!`" After that, how could I refuse? A sleek, cream coloured cat with brown ears and paws and the bluest of eyes joined the family, and the latest arrival was so beautiful that I couldn't help loving her. When ever I wrote letters home she jealously jumped up and tried to sit on the letter.

Over the six months of Guy's absence I was supported by radio contact with the doctors at Mvumi. George, the farm manager and his wife Joan were a tower of strength. Our Tanzanian lay-preachers, Michael, Yoram, and Yusufu led Sunday services in the centre's chapel.

The patients conducted their own Evening Prayers in the hospital, or outside on the patio, and their enthusiastic singing could be heard from far away. If I felt lonely in the evenings I often joined them. A woman whose leg had been amputated due to a malignant ulcer did not have long to live. She was a widow, and all six of her children had died in infancy (not uncommon when she was young!) "Mama," I said to her one day, "you've been listening to the patients preaching right outside your room every evening. What do you think? Do you want Jesus to be your Saviour?"

Ndio! she said. "Yes!" She wanted to be baptised, and her baptism took place in her room the following week. "Now I can die happy," she told me in Swahili, "because I'm going to be with Jesus when I leave this world. Just think, if I hadn't come here, I would never have had the chance!"

A friend in Australia, Pastor Roy Halcrowe, sent me a

leaflet entitled *Why was Jesus born in a barn?* The answer was, *Because he was the Lamb of God.* When I was asked to give a talk for patients and staff gathered on the lawn to celebrate Christmas, I used the impelling words of this little tract.

The baby Jesus was born to be the Lamb of God, it said, because he was to die as a sacrifice for the sins of the world. He was born in an inn-keeper's animal hut, (beside the domestic animals, some of which must have been kept by the inn-keeper for sacrifice for his own and his family's sins) It was appropriate that the first people called to see the newborn Lamb of God were shepherds, caring for sheep and lambs on the hillside outside Bethlehem.

An elderly patient was deeply touched by the message. "If Jesus came as a little baby in order to die for me," he told Yusufu afterwards, "I want him to be my Saviour." He too wanted to be baptised, and for a baptismal name he chose that of "Abraham." On the day of his discharge from hospital he came to say goodbye to me, and thanked me for helping him to find Jesus as his Saviour.

Of all the places where I'd worked, I loved Hombolo the best.

—•◆•—

I loved to go on safari with Guy and Dawn when Guy went to see patients at government dispensaries. Invariably we would stop under a baobab tree for lunch, and Guy would get out the fold-up table and chairs, and set them up in the shade. Dawn always covered the table with a dainty cloth, and put out serviettes to match. When we were seated, Guy would remove his hat in deference to God's presence, then reverently say grace, replacing his hat when he finished.

Our conversation always included some of Guy's jokes with which he entertained not only us, but also his patients when ever he did hospital rounds. Laughter always lightened the lot of those whose lives Guy touched.

When Guy and Dawn retired, Brian and Sue with their three sons took their place. Brian instigated visits from the Flying Doctor Service to bring specialist surgeons from Nairobi to reconstruct damaged hands. Angela, an English physiotherapist, came to teach these patients to use their hands again. She and I shared house.

Patients who suffered amputation due to chronic leg ulcers had to either crawl along the ground or use crutches. One man, afraid of amputation, stayed at home until his leg became gangrenous. He finally crawled to the leprosy centre to submit to amputation and as he thought to lose his self respect forever. But Brian was experimenting with fibreglass legs, and succeeded in making them. He taught the art to Yusufu, who was then able to construct them in the shoemaking room. Patients who had lost their self respect regained it as they learned to walk again.

After only one year, Angela, with whom I'd so happily shared house, developed a muscular illness and had to return to England, and was greatly missed. Isobel, a retired Scottish doctor came to help. Everywhere she went she took her big black umbrella and her big black dog, Whisky. When she went away for a week she inadvertently left her umbrella in my house and Whisky lay down beside it, his nose along his paws, looking up mournfully at me, refusing to move until his mistress came home. I enjoyed Isobel's friendship, and when she left I missed her very much. She and Angela had been the only other single missionaries.

We were joined by Jean, an Australian widow, grandmother of ten, who came to give three years voluntary service with The Leprosy Mission, as hospital administrator. Small children crowded around her, talking in Cigogo. She answered them in English, and if neither understood what the other was saying it didn't matter, for it was the language of love, and all understood that. She was able to do what I couldn't do – to cut out and sew warm capes for the nurses. God had made up the deficiency!

The Adams family adopted Jean as instant grandmother for their children, and she continued in that role until they went home on leave. Guy and Dawn returned to relieve the Adams, and Guy was not very pleased with some of the changes that had been made in his absence. He quickly changed things back to the way they were.

Rainbirds were making their hollow booming calls and frogs and scorpions began coming out after torrential rain, when a scorpion bit me through my open sandal. It was my third scorpion bite since coming to Africa. I remembered the first, at language school, seventeen years before. I'd been thirty-three then, and now I was fifty. I'd learnt, in language school, that the things that sting in life can sometimes be very painful, but ultimately can teach us something we need to learn. Hurt pride had been my problem then, and my pride was about to be stung again, and it would hurt – terribly.

Misunderstandings occurred more and more frequently, and finally something happened that caused me to feel rejected. My pride was hurt, and when we tried to talk things over I didn't accept the explanation given, nor the other person's attempt to make up the quarrel. I forgot the important lesson God had taught me at Mvumi, that elephants may never forget, but humans have to! Once more I was miserable, and it was my own fault, but this time I nursed the grievance, and gave up all hope of reconciliation.

A week's holiday was due to me, and I spent it at Mvumi. There I read a book about an English woman of the previous century whose father had been a trader in West Africa. When he died she took over the business, and for many years travelled alone amongst the African people. The story made me remember how happy I'd been at Kalinzi and in the Mvumi village clinics, working only with Africans. If I could do that sort of work again, I thought, there'd be no more misunderstandings between myself and my fellow missionaries.

My job was due to be nationalised after my next leave, and I'd then be moving on. Kneeling down, I told God that if it was his will, I was willing to work alone amongst the African people again. Then, feeling that something constructive had been done, I stopped worrying.

Before going home on leave I made another serious error. I'd always left it to the Bishop to appoint my place of service, believing God to be his guide. Now, for the first time, I didn't trust God enough to leave my future in his hands. Instead, feeling out of touch with general hospital work after more than seven years away, I pleaded with our African Bishop, Yohanna Madinda, not to send me back to a hospital but rather to some kind of community health work in the villages.

I didn't know what I was asking. Within the diocese there was no other project like the Mvumi mobile clinics, which were now fully nationalised. God had always in the past enabled me to cope with any job he had given me. Why had I lost my trust?

I could not have imagined the serious consequences that would occur as a result of my refusal to make up our quarrel. Not realising that I had done anything wrong, I went home on leave.

Chapter 22

Deeply distressed because relationships were not as they should have been between me and my fellow workers, I remember that leave mainly because of the tears I shed.

For the first time no-one was there to meet me when I returned to Tanzania. Trying not to feel bereft, I begged a lift from Dodoma airfield into town and went to Mackay House to report to the Bishop. He was surprised to see me, and apologetic. Something had gone wrong with communications, he said, and he had not been informed of my arrival date.

"You should go back to Hombolo and pack up." he advised. "When the new A-grade male nurse arrives you'll be going to Kondoa. It's a town of seventeen thousand people, mostly Muslims, half way to Arusha. There's a pastor, and your house is in the same compound as his. You will have to find a way to get out to the villages to start some form of low key medical work. I'm sorry I have no car to give you."

Back at Hombolo I stood gazing out the window at the familiar scene. Would I forever be moving on? I remembered the words of Psalm 90, written by Moses, who never had a permanent home on this earth. *Lord, thou hast been our dwelling-place in all generations. Psalm 90:1 RSV*

On arrival at Kondoa I was welcomed by the pastor and his wife and children, but I missed the light-hearted banter of my fellow missionaries. I didn't know any of the Africans, not even the pastor. I was a stranger in a strange place.

My life as a nurse had always revolved around a hospital where every one knew every one else, and there had been a set routine for every day. Now I had to work out my own routine. Instead of focussing on caring for other people, I had to focus on caring for myself! I'd always inherited well-trained house boys and a hospital vehicle for doing the shopping, but now I had to walk to market every day, buy and carry my own supplies and do my own cooking. I could have hired a house servant, but I was afraid to do so until I got to know a suitable and trustworthy person. The only opportunity I found to communicate the gospel was when a Masai called in on his way to the cattle-market, and I set out for the market myself with a bag of Swahili tracts. I never got there – the tracts were so popular they'd all gone before I'd walked a mile!

Kondoa had a large government hospital, so there was no opening for medical work in the town. To start some kind of low key medical work as the Bishop suggested meant finding a way to get out to the villages. But how? One day I heard the Pastor complaining loudly to a visitor that the Bishop had sent him a missionary but no car for her to get around in. I decided to return to Dodoma and plead with the Bishop for a car.

The Pastor arranged for a youth to join the crowd waiting for the bus, to try and get a seat for me. He succeeded, but the journey was fruitless. The Bishop had no car to give me.

One month later I tried again. This time the Pastor was away, so I walked to the main road and joined a group of Africans waiting there since sunrise in the hope of a lift from any passing truck. Eventually one pulled up, and the Africans made a deal with the Indian driver and climbed up a narrow ladder on the side of the vehicle. But when I tried to do the same, the driver stopped me. The vehicle was not supposed to carry passengers and he was afraid to take a European on board. But I continued to plead, and at last he took my fare. Climbing the ladder I found a place amongst the bags of rice, like the men. Whenever we passed through towns, the men lay low in case the police saw them, and I followed their example. The fact that our ride was illegal made no difference to me. I felt desperate to get to Dodoma and see the Bishop. Somehow, I had to find a way to get out to the villages and commence work. Heavy rain began, and we sheltered under the tarpaulin with which the driver covered the rice. Under the canvas cover I had my first discussion of the gospel since coming to Kondoa, and realised that sharing the lot of the ordinary people was what opened the way for deeper communication.

But once more the Bishop had no car to give me. I returned to Kondoa, wondering whether he might be hoping I could appeal to friends in Australia to provide one. That's impossible, I thought, and I didn't know what to do.

The only things that moved in the house were a stream of ants that scurried up and down the door-jamb, and the slowly moving water that leaked from the toilet overnight, and met me, like an old acquaintance, at the bend of the hallway every morning. The trees surrounding the house engulfed it in shadow long before the sun set. Behind the banana grove lay the town's tree nursery, watered by irrigation from a large spring. From the irrigation system each night came the croaking of hundreds of frogs, which normally I would have enjoyed, but now it seemed to be a melancholy sound.

Friday, in a Muslim town, was begging day. As the only white woman in the area I felt vulnerable, and made up my mind I would not give to beggars unless I could see they were really genuine. The first beggar who came to my door was a young man who seemed to be not quite normal mentally. Because of this, I decided to give to him regularly, but also to find something for him to do. There were leaves to be swept up and the grass to cut, so he became my garden-boy, and his regular coming each day was a comfort to me.

The second beggar who came was a little old man, and I thought of my little old mother, and for her sake I accepted him and told him he could come every Friday.

The third beggar had only one hand – his left. The right had been amputated at the wrist. He was clean and decently dressed, and the Pastor told me he had grandsons who helped him, and that he had chickens and goats. He doesn't need my help I decided, and I told him not to come again.

But he came. Each time I gave him a cup of coffee, but no money.

"The lady who lived here before you was just like my own mother," he protested. Well, why didn't you believe her when she told you about Jesus? I muttered under my breath. I'm not going to be your mother, Bwana!

Briefly, but with a hard edge to my voice I did my duty and explained the gospel to him, but I gave him no money. As he walked away I thought, This is terrible. I've tried to explain the gospel to him, but instead of love in my heart there was utter rejection! I sensed that I had done something terribly wrong. The gospel should only ever be explained in love.

Then something happened. Things were not the same any more between God and me. It was like the time when I'd refused the peace-offering of my flat-mate at Mvumi years before. Every time I opened my Bible, words not of comfort but of God's anger and rebuke met my gaze. I was a disgrace to my God and it seemed he might be about to throw me out of the country!

God had really got my attention now. I asked his forgiveness for the way I'd treated the beggar. The following Friday morning I got up early and went out and sat under a tree on the side of the road where people passed as they came walking into town with their produce to sell at the market. After two hours I saw him coming – the one handed beggar. I told him how sorry I was for speaking so angrily, and told him he could come every Friday if he wanted to. He said that he did not want to beg, but would bring eggs or a chicken to sell to me. We parted friends.

Now I had two friends in Kondoa – my garden boy and the one-handed beggar! I hoped that God had forgiven me, but two weeks later as I bent over the wash tub and saw some small, brown blobs skating about in the vision of my right eye, my conscience smote me. They were still there the next day, now in both eyes, and they didn't go away. Had God's judgement come upon me at last? I was afraid.

The pilot of the MAF plane was able to pick me up at Kondoa airstrip and fly me to Moshi to see the eye specialist at Kilimanjaro Christian Medical Centre. Although it was late in the day when I arrived, Dr Marilyn Scudder took me to the hospital and examined my eyes patiently and thoroughly. The vitreous tissue inside the eye had torn, she said, but the nerve of sight, the retina, was intact. The "floaters" – those tiny fragments skating about in my vision, were harmless. I thanked her for her kindness, and I thanked God for his mercy to me, and promised to try and be kinder to beggars.

Jean, the sister I'd relieved at Berega who was now on the staff of KCMC, invited me to stay with her. "Why don't you have that indigestion seen to while you're here?" she suggested, hearing an explosive burp after dinner.

"I've had the problem for years." I replied. "I just take a

bit of Mag. Trisil and it fixes it."

"You should have it seen to while you're here." she insisted. "You might have a stomach ulcer." To please her I went to the outpatients' next day. "We'll put a tube down tomorrow and have a look" the doctor said, and the following day I underwent an examination. Out of the mists of sedation I heard a voice urging, "Swallow! Swallow!" but trying to swallow felt like trying to swallow a bunch of knives. "There seems to be some obstruction here," the voice remarked, and then my throat was bathed with merciful fluid and I drifted back to sleep. I awoke in a hospital bed.

"Why didn't you tell me that you had difficulty in swallowing?" the doctor asked when he came in.

"I didn't know I had," I replied truthfully. "I just thought I had a small throat." A memory came back of trying unsuccessfully to swallow a piece of meat a few months previously, and having to regurgitate it.

"We'll try again tomorrow, under general anaesthetic," he said. They did, but still the tube wouldn't go down. "Your throat is very swollen now. You'll have to go home and wait until all the swelling has gone before we can try again," he said. "You should come back in one month's time. We must find out the cause of the obstruction."

My throat was so painful I could scarcely swallow. I'll never go back for them to do this to me again, I exploded! One night the cold air seeped in through the open shutters and I awoke feeling as if my throat was being obstructed. Panic gripped me. Was I going to choke, all alone? Lighting a lantern, I knelt down beside my bed and opened a small devotional book entitled *God Calling*, asking God to speak to me. I read: *He came from above, He took me, He drew me out of many waters. 2 Samuel 22:17*

Next I opened my Bible, and the words that confronted me were the same words as in *God Calling,* in a slightly different translation:

He reached from on high, he took me .... he drew me out of many waters. 2 Samuel 22:17 RSV

Now I was sure God was speaking to me, and I calmed down and all fear vanished. Finding a hot-water-bag, I filled it and propping up more pillows I went back to bed holding the warm bag against my throat. Every night I did the same, and gradually the swollen tissue in my throat subsided. Finally I was able to swallow again without pain.

Now I tried hard to be obedient to God in every way. The war in Uganda between Idi Amin and his opponents was costing Tanzania money and troops, and commodities such as flour and sugar were rationed. As I tried to practise sharing without fear, my supply of sugar finished. When it was all gone I breathed a sigh of relief. I felt free! I had obeyed, and it didn't matter that there was none left. Now I'm like everyone else, I thought, and it was a relief not to be a source of supply, just for a while.

But I'd forgotten one thing. When I needed to make bread, the recipe said to put one teaspoon of sugar into the flour to activate the yeast. Now I would have to be like others, and beg. Calling on the pastor, I asked him, "Could you please let me have me one teaspoon of sugar, if you have any?"

"You can have your share of a whole sack of sugar." he replied. "I've just managed to get one from the co-operative shop."

A whole sack of sugar! And I could have my share! I could hardly believe it. Jesus' promise came to my mind:

Give, and it will be given to you; good measure, pressed

down, shaken together, running over, will be put into your lap. For the measure you give will be the measure you get back. Luke 6:38 RSV

God was teaching me that when we obey him and share what we have, our own needs will be supplied.

Chapter 23

Suddenly the opportunity I'd been waiting for came – a chance to get out to a village, to do some medical work. A Missionary Aviation Fellowship plane was coming to test an air strip so that it could bring medical aid and pastoral care to remote villages. The pilot would pick up the pastor and me with a local government official, drop us all at Mwailange airstrip, and return for us before sunset.

Flying low over the airstrip, we could see people below waving excitedly. Joy filled my heart for this was the work I'd come to do. After a trial run the pilot turned and came in to land, and the people who had made the air-strip jubilantly escorted us to their village. The sick were already lining up at the small church which was to be used as a clinic. All day they continued to come, some having walked long distances.

At the end of the day I joined the crowd waiting for the plane to return. With me were two children, twelve-year-old Agnes and her two-year-old brother, Soko. The little boy's light coloured hair and match-stick arms and legs revealed severe malnutrition. Their mother had died, and their father had left them with relatives and had gone. Agnes, who had been appointed carer for her little brother, was doing her best, but it was obvious that without proper feeding he would soon die. Their uncle readily gave permission for me to take them to an orphanage in Moshi and leave them there until the little boy reached the nutritional safety of four years of age.

But there was one problem. The plane was already full. Nevertheless, we waited in hope, praying that somehow the children might be able to accompany us. The plane did not come and the sun set. Darkness fell, and the church teacher's daughter who had adopted me as her friend joyfully took me home to spend the night. In the morning we continued our vigil, but there was no sign of the plane. Around midday the sound of a motor was heard. The pilot had been unable to return, and a government Land Rover had come for us. We were able to squeeze the children in, and I thanked God for his solution to their dilemma.

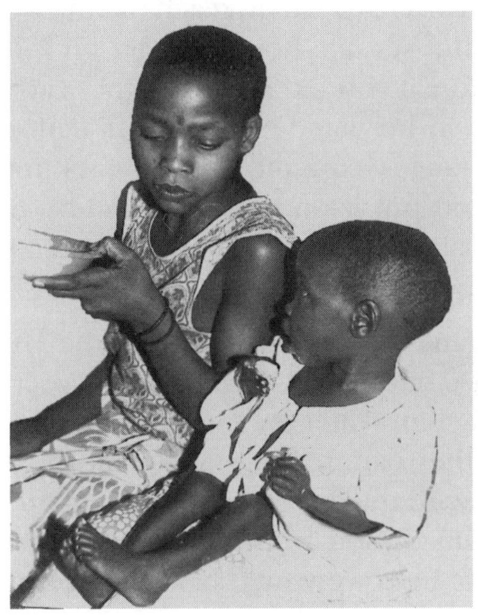

Agnes and Soko, Tanzania 1980

Neither of the children had ever seen a bath before, but they eagerly climbed in. Agnes bathed herself, while I scrubbed Soko, then lifted him out and dried him. There were children's clothes from Australia, but nothing to fit a twelve-year-old girl. Agnes's eyes shone as I wrapped half my sarong with pretty mauve flowers around her. She washed the black cloth she had been wearing and hung it out to dry. After eating, they climbed into bed in the guest-room, and that night I went to sleep happy. A verse from the Bible came to my mind: *He gives the barren woman a home, making her the joyous mother of children. Psalm 113:9 RSV* Even if only for a few days, Agnes and Soko had changed my life, just as Mapenzi had done at Berega.

The time had come for my next throat examination, and American friends had promised to take me to Moshi with them by car. First, I had to reach their town by bus. We got up early and set out, hoping to get on the bus at the main road before it entered Kondoa. Agnes carried Soko on her back, and in her hand a few things tied in her black cloth. Before long, seeing me tire, she took my overnight bag as well and put it on her head, and by the time we reached the main road we were both glad to sit in the shade of a roadside booth and rest.

As we drank tea and ate samousas the Muslim booth keeper asked where I was taking the children. I had just finished telling him when the bus swept round the corner. He ran onto the road, waving madly, and held a shouted conversation with the driver, then shepherded us onto the bus. How I thanked God for the kind Muslim booth keeper, without whose help we would have been left standing on the road.

Back in Kondoa the crowd surged on, and I breathed a sigh of relief that we were already seated. Two hours late, we arrived in the town where the American missionaries lived. Would someone still be waiting? Yes, there was my friend's husband, standing amongst the crowd. He did not mind adding two children to his safari, and drove us home to spend the night. Agnes's eyes grew wide with wonder at the generous meal set out on a snowy tablecloth. Night fell, and we were directed to a king-sized bed which was amply big enough for the three of us. Soko slept soundly while Agnes and I whispered to each other until we fell asleep.

The sun was setting as we drove into Moshi next day, the snow on Mt Kilimanjaro reflecting rose pink in the evening light. Our friends dropped us at Bethel Orphanage, which was administered by the Brethren Church. It was situated next to Kilimanjaro Christian Medical Centre. After admitting the children I walked across to KCMC to Jean's house. Wendy, with whom I'd shared house at Berega was now teaching at KCMC school, and she was coming to dinner. We all shared our news, and the next morning I reported to the hospital for the repeat examination. When I awoke Wendy was sitting beside me, and she excused herself as Dr Welles Hannah came into the room. He sat down beside my bed.

"Well, Jo, you'll be pleased to know that this time they got the tube down," he said cheerfully. "There's no actual obstruction there. The reason the tube wouldn't go down the first time was oesophageal spasm, caused by long-standing emotional stress." He paused to allow time for his words to sink in. After a few minutes he continued. "Two other doctors and I have discussed this very carefully, Jo, and we've come to the conclusion that there's only one way for you to get better. You'll have to go home to Australia."

My world fell apart. It was a death sentence to all I'd loved and lived for.

"But I've only been back a few months, and if I'm sent home now because of an emotional illness, you know what will happen," I protested. "CMS will never let me come back! Besides, I'm much better now. The stress is all behind me!"

Welles shook his head. "You have difficulty in

swallowing, Jo." he said. "Normal European foods are hard to come by. They're already rationed due to the war in Uganda with Idi Amin, and it's going to get worse. Much worse."

"But God called me to this country," I pleaded. "He's always enabled me to cope. He brought me to Kondoa, and I'm just getting used to it!"

"Even Moses was not allowed to enter the promised land," Welles said with finality. "He was allowed to see it, but not to enter it."

My heart filled with sorrow. God had allowed me to see my promised land from the air, to taste the joy of one medical air safari, to save the life of one little boy, but I was not to be allowed to continue the work. The warning I'd feared that God had given me, that he was going to send me right out of this country, was being fulfilled. Like Job, the thing that I greatly feared had come upon me. *(Job 3:25)*

I dressed and returned to Jean's house. She was still on duty, so I was able to be alone. No tears came. Numb with shock, I sat down on the lounge, trying to comprehend the enormity of what was happening. A book was lying on the table, and I picked it up and opened it. It was by an author of whom I'd never heard – Carlo Carretto – and was entitled *The God Who Comes*. I began to read, and immediately I knew that the book was meant to be there, and I was meant to see it. It had the same message in it that God had given me eighteen years before, when medical reasons had cast doubt on my fitness for overseas service. Through Jessie Penn Lewis's book, *Dying to Live*, I'd learnt that when our will conflicts with God's will we must allow God to choose, even if it means dying to our own dearest ambition. By dying to self we live for God, and this is the only way of blessing. Here, in Carlo Carretto's words, I found the same message:

I now saw that by teaching me this truth before he allowed me to leave my own country and come to this land, God had prepared me for the time when, against my own wishes, I would have to go home.

There in the Lord's presence, I accepted his will. If God wanted me to go home I accepted it. Closing the book, I put it back on the table and went outside. There was a little track leading in amongst the trees, and I followed it down to a stream of clear water, fed by the snows above. Removing my sandals, I immersed my feet in the icy water and waded. Then, refreshed, I walked barefoot through the lush grass, following the stream. Higher up, the water was tumultuous, rushing swiftly over the rocks.

Turning, I walked downstream again, and came to a place where the stream was wide and deep and quiet. Here the water scarcely seemed to be moving. Sitting on a rock, I contemplated the phenomenon. The same stream here gave the impression of being unmoving, but higher up I'd seen it tumbling over the rocks at a frantic pace.

It must be because it's deeper here that it seems not to be moving, I thought. Up there where the water is racing madly the stream must be very shallow. As I sat meditating, the stream seemed to be an illustration of what was happening to me. Over the past eighteen years my life had been tempestuous, rushing from place to place, like the rocky part of the stream. Now I was going home to still waters that perhaps might scarcely seem to be moving, but they would be moving deep down underneath because it was the same stream. It seemed to symbolise the river of the Holy Spirit flowing out from God. We were all part of it, those who serve overseas and those who serve at home.

Whether we were in the fast water or the slow, it was the same river of the Holy Spirit flowing out into the world.

Suddenly I noticed that evening shadows were filling the glen, and I stood up to leave. As I did so, I saw that high above, on the mountain, the sun was still shining. I'm entering the shadows, I thought, but the sun is still shining up above. Perhaps the sun will shine for me again some day.

The bus took me all the way back to Dodoma, and I went straight to see the Bishop, preceding the doctor's letter with the news that I had to go home. At first he refused to accept it, believing that if he moved me back to Dodoma to the company of my fellow missionaries I would get better. I was sent back to Kondoa to pack up, while he tried to reverse the doctor's decision.

I'd promised to come back and see the children. When Agnes saw me coming, she ran and flung her arms around me, but was very sad when I told her that I was sick and had to go home. I encouraged her to stay in the orphanage, explaining that the pastor at Kondoa had promised that when Soko was big enough he would come and take them home. They were very happy there, and Soko was already looking better. I would never forget them.

Returning to Kondoa, I packed my household equipment in my green tin trunk and padlocked it. It would await the diocesan truck. If I didn't come back it would assist some new missionaries until their own equipment arrived. My American friends had promised to collect me on their way back to Dodoma, and my packing was finished just in time. It had been raining, and as we left Kondoa the last thing I saw was a double rainbow arching over the wet countryside. It brought to my mind some words from the Book of Revelation:

At once I was in the Spirit, and lo, a throne stood in heaven, with one seated on the throne!.....and round about the throne was a rainbow that looked like an emerald.
Revelation 4:2,3 RSV

A tiny Commentary on Daily Light that I'd found in my house at Hombolo had this to say about those verses:

"The throne of God's judgement is surrounded by the rainbow of God's mercy."

I'm experiencing God's judgement now, I thought. Perhaps, sometime in the future, in God's time, I'll also experience his mercy.

In the months to come I would passionately pray that God would bring many people to Christ in the villages surrounding Kondoa, and in the years ahead missionaries from New Zealand would come and show the Jesus video very widely in that region, and God's Holy Spirit would bring many people to Christ. Part of the blessing for me would be that the one who wrote and told me of the blessing when it came would be one from whom at the time of my departure I was estranged. That he took the trouble to write and tell me about God's blessing falling on the Kondoa region would assure me that our relationship was finally healed.

Back at Dodoma, my friends, Brian and Sue, who had moved from Hombolo to work in Dodoma because of their children's schooling, welcomed me into their household while Bishop Madinda continued to try to reverse the doctors' decision. But at the end of six weeks it became clear that nothing could change things. It was not only the doctors' decision, I believed, but God's.

In my Bible I read, *"We know that in everything God works for good with those who love him, who are called according to his purpose." Romans 8:28 RSV*

I knew that *"in everything"* included this, and Carlo Carretto's words continued to bring me consolation, *"that it is at the moment of our death to self that God's blessing is burst open to flow for us."*

I flew to Dar es Salaam and Janet, now stationed there, met me at the airport and took me to her apartment. In the morning she drove me to the overseas air terminal. As the jet took off, I looked down and back at the coast of Tanzania, rapidly disappearing in the haze between sky and ocean, until only an empty expanse remained. Three questions occupied my mind:

Would I ever come back to Africa?

How had I come to this day of crisis in my life?

What was ahead for me?

It would not be until I reached Australia that God would give me the answers.

Chapter 24

The chortling of currawongs awoke me, and slowly I opened my eyes and looked around my sister's guest room where I'd slept. The devastating truth hit me. I'd been sent home from Tanzania!

The house was quiet. It was early Sunday morning and everyone was still asleep. I went quietly out to the kitchen, made a cup of coffee and switched the radio on softly. The morning 2CH devotional was just starting. It was the story of a man who owned a small shop but did not have the money to pay the mortgage, which had fallen due. He made an appointment with the bank manager.

"You and I have been friends for a long time." the manager told him." I'm personally going to pay this debt off for you. Come in and see me in a couple of weeks and the papers will be ready to sign. Then the shop will be yours."

The man could scarcely believe his good fortune. After two weeks he returned, expectantly. The bank manager took out the papers. "Here they are," he said, "all ready." Then he tore the papers up in front of him.

"What – what are you doing?" the man stammered.

"I've closed you down, mate. I was ready to pay off that debt for you, but I heard how you went out from this office and demanded payment of a small debt from a friend. I've closed you down, mate, and what's more, when you get home you'll find a padlock on the door!"

It was a modern version of Jesus' parable of the unforgiving debtor. (*Matthew 18:23-35*) As the story ended

I saw my hand snapping shut the padlock on my green tin trunk back in Tanzania. In that instant I believed I knew why God had sent me home. I'd felt rejected, and had given up trying to be reconciled, and had asked God to send me far away, where there could be no more misunderstandings. As I listened to the radio story, the sword of the word of God cut deep into my soul and I saw for the first time that I had not forgiven my fellow missionaries. The words I'd just heard echoed in my mind with terrible finality – *"I've closed you down, mate, and what's more, when you get home you'll find a padlock on the door."*

The Lord brought me to a beautiful place where I could be quiet and sort out my life. Two months after arriving home I noticed that the deaconess of the village where my mother lived was not there any more. "She resigned," someone told me, "and they still haven't found a replacement." Unable to face nursing in Australia after eighteen years away, I remembered how much I'd enjoyed deaconess training and I applied for the vacant position. I was accepted, initially as a Parish Sister, and was given a flat on the fifth floor of the same building in which my mother lived. From my balcony I looked out over green fields and tree tops where birds swooped in evening revelry. The chaplains and residents of the village took me to their hearts, and I found the warm acceptance and friendship I'd been longing for.

There was time for quiet reflection, and as I looked back I saw that from childhood it had been my habit to hide my real feelings when hurt, and to run away from those who hurt me. My years of living in community had been years of retreating from those with whom I differed, and it had led to a habit of cutting myself off from the social life of my own culture, which in turn led to a growing sense of isolation.

I loved my new work, and marvelled that in spite of all my faults and failures, God brought me right into the sanctuary of his church, to administer the cup representing Jesus' blood in the Service of Holy Communion.

But in spite of all God gave me I continued to grieve over the loss of Tanzania. One day I went to see the Rev Peter Dawson, the Overseas Secretary of CMS. Did I have any chance of returning, to Tanzania I asked him? "I don't see why not, Jo, if you're well enough," Peter replied encouragingly, and he suggested I go to see one of the CMS honorary doctors.

I followed his suggestion, and the doctor gave his candid opinion.

"Look at your hands, Jo," he said. I looked down, and saw that all the time I'd been talking my fingers had been twisting and untwisting with emotion. The next time I went to see him I kept my hands in my pockets! But after that I didn't go any more. What's the use, I thought hopelessly. I was told I'd find a padlock on the door.

I'd believed my missionary call was for life, yet now all seemed to be over. As I grieved and wept and blamed myself, one day it seemed as if I were entering a great black hole without one ray of light. It was then that I knew I must make a choice. Either I could accept God's forgiveness and get on with the work he had given me, or I could refuse God's forgiveness and the new life he was offering me. I chose to accept his mercy and get on with my job. But despite my good intentions, I found my mind going over the unhappy events of the past.

One of my duties was to take my place on the preaching roster, and I wanted to speak on how God not only forgives, he also forgets. But nowhere in my Bible

Concordance could I find any reference to say that God forgets. Instead, I found God says: *"I will forgive their iniquity, and I will remember their sin no more." Jeremiah 31:34 RSV* Of course, I thought, God can't forget, because forgetting is accidental. God knows everything. It's a matter of the will. God says that he *will* not remember. Every time I dwelt on what someone had said or done that had hurt me I was reminding God of something he did not wish to remember. What God refused to remember, I must refuse to recall!

But it was more easily said than done. An illustration from the Old Testament helped me. *Thou wilt cast all our sins into the depths of the sea. Micah 7:19 RSV*

On my way to the city by train one morning an unhappy memory began to surface in my mind, and as the train sped over the Harbour Bridge I took that unhappy memory and dropped it over the side of the bridge. In my imagination I watched it fall, down, down, and hit the water with a splash, then disappear beneath the waves. I never allowed that memory to re-surface, and after a while I forgot what it had been all about. If Satan, who is called in Revelation 12:10 the accuser of the brethren, continued to accuse my Christian brothers and sisters to me, I now told him in the Name of Christ to go! And he did. I wrote to those with whom I'd had differences and asked their forgiveness. A letter of apology came back that brought lasting reconciliation.

As I rejoiced in our new-found reconciliation, a letter arrived from Tanzania with shattering news. Mama Bilha, the hospital chaplain at Kilimatinde, had died in tragic circumstances. Like many Africans, the nurses' home house-mother usually slept with a lighted lantern in her room. One night she smelt gas and went to investigate, her lantern in her hand. Escaping gas from a leaking cylinder met her and the resulting explosion blew the roof off the kitchen. Mama Bilha received third degree burns. The nurses were deeply moved by her courage and her faith in God. She prayed that her son would get there before she died, but it was not to be. Three days later, before her son could be contacted, she passed away. Her faith in God had remained unshakeable to the end.

I was devastated, and also mystified. "Lord, how could you allow such a terrible thing to happen to your faithful servant, I asked?

My copy of the "The Living Bible" was lying on the table beside me as I asked, and I opened it. The passage on the page at which I had opened was well known to me in the King James Version of the Bible, where it says, *"God is our refuge and strength, a very present help in trouble. Therefore we will not fear, though the earth should change, though the mountains shake in the heart of the sea." Psalm 46:1,2 RSV*

But in the paraphrase of The Living Bible, the same passage used a modern illustration to express the same truth:

"Even if the world blows up, yet will I trust Him." Psalm 46:2 Living Bible.

Mama Bilha's world had indeed blown up, but she had trusted God to the end. And that, I thought, is just what we all hope we'll be enabled to do.

I was greatly comforted.

But over the sin of my own former unforgiving attitude, I still continued to grieve. Then, just as God had comforted me regarding Mama Bilha's death, he now began to comfort me regarding my own personal sorrow. I read in the New Testament:

"My son, do not regard lightly the discipline of the Lord,
nor lose courage when you are punished by him.
For the Lord disciplines him whom he loves,
and chastises every son whom he receives."
Hebrews 12:5-6 RSV

I had never really understood what it meant to have God as my Father, but now I began to understand. God had disciplined me because he loved me and wanted me to repent, so that he could forgive me.

I came to the conclusion that even if we lose the thing we love the most, if we still have God as our Father, we have everything.

He heals the broken hearted and binds up their wounds, says Psalm 147 verse 3. Slowly God was healing my broken heart and binding up my wounds, as he promised. Some gracious words from the Book of Isaiah amazed me the most, revealing God's great humility, as well as his love:

For thus says the high and lofty One who inhabits eternity, whose name is Holy:"I dwell in the high and holy place, and also with him who is of a contrite and humble spirit, to revive the spirit of the humble, and to revive the heart of the contrite." Isaiah 57:15 RSV

At the end of my first year at home Bishop Donald Robinson accepted me for ordination as a deaconess. It had been raining, and as I drove down Epping Road after the interview, a beautiful rainbow arched across the city of Sydney. I remembered the double rainbow that had arched over the rainy countryside of Kondoa, the last place where I'd worked in Tanzania, the day I left. The words of my *Daily Light* commentary had said:

"The throne of God's judgement is surrounded by the rainbow of God's mercy."

God's judgement had caused me to leave Tanzania, but God's mercy had reinstated me as his servant here at home. I was deeply, deeply grateful.

But I still had one question. Would God ever take me back to Africa?

Chapter 25

They thought it was all over," said the retired minister in his Easter sermon, speaking of two disciples on the road from Jerusalem to Emmaus after the crucifixion and death of Jesus. "They had thought they would always be with him," he continued, "but now he was dead, and their own work, which they had thought was just beginning, was ended. The dispirited, dejected disciples had given up hope and were going home.

But it was not all over! Not by a long shot, it wasn't! There was a world out there to be won to Christ, and they were to have a part in winning it!"

Something stirred within me as I listened. A faint hope was born in my heart. Perhaps for me, too, it was not all over, after all? Could God be telling me that he might one day yet restore to me that which he had taken away?

A third year passed slowly by. One Sunday another retired minister preached on the exile of the Israelites in Babylon. "They thought the exile was for ever," he said. "No, it was not to be forever. It was just for a time. Seventy years, to be exact. After they repented, God would bring them back to their land."

Could my exile from the land I loved also be just for a time? Would God take me back? Was God speaking to me? The flame of hope burned a little more brightly in my heart. I read: *May the God of hope fill you with all joy and peace in believing, so that by the power of the Holy Spirit you may abound in hope. Romans 15:13 RSV*

Easter was approaching again, my fourth year home, and the chaplain in charge said that each chapel in the Village should have one person to give a series of addresses through Holy Week. I couldn't resist asking whether I was to be one of those rostered. "Yes, you too." he promised.

It was the first time I'd given a consecutive series of addresses, and when some of the congregation expressed their appreciation I felt encouraged. Perhaps this is to be my calling now, I thought, no longer overseas missionary work but deaconess work here at home? But when Easter Day came, a very senior retired clergyman led the service, and I felt embarrassed that I, not he, should be rostered to preach the sermon. After the service I told him how I felt.

"I was glad to have you do it, dear." he replied graciously. "I didn't know how I was going to get through the service." Did he really feel that sick, I wondered, or was he just being kind?

That night I had a dream. I was sitting at the chaplain's desk, writing. The chaplain came in and said in his courteous and kind manner, *You can go back to your own office now, Jo.* Feeling embarrassed, I got up and went back to my own office. As I did so, I realised that the work I'd been doing was finished, and there would be no more need for me to sit at the Chaplain's desk. At that moment my radio clock woke me with the Rev Arthur Dean's 6am Bible Study.

Jesus went to dine at the house of a ruler and he noticed how guests chose for themselves the seats of honour. He told this parable:

When you are invited by any one to a marriage feast, do not sit down in a place of honour, lest a more eminent man than you be invited by him; and he who invited you both will come and say to you, 'Give place to this man,' and then you will begin with shame to take the lowest place.

.....For every one who exalts himself will be humbled, and he who humbles himself will be exalted." Luke 14:7-11

I told the chaplain that I didn't want to be on the preaching roster any more. God had, I believed, shown me that the clergy's gift was not mine, and I wanted them to have their rightful preaching opportunities. In my dream I'd been told, *"You can go back to your own office, now, Jo."* What was my office? It was that of a missionary.

How could I do the work of a missionary here at home, I wondered? I asked God to show me.

As I parked my car by the side of the road in the shopping centre one evening, I noticed an attractive young woman explaining some leaflets to two teenage girls, who were listening attentively. Another young woman stood nearby, holding more leaflets and obviously praying.

"I didn't know people would listen if you did this sort of thing here in Australia, I thought, astonished. Perhaps this was a way I could be a missionary here at home! Who could I ask to go with me? The face of Rae Croft, our minister's wife, came before me.

Rae was delighted. The following Thursday night we began at the entrance to the largest shopping complex in the city of Parramatta. The first person I spoke to brushed me aside. The second remarked breezily, "I do the same as you for the Catholic church," and hurried on. Feeling like running away, I went to tell Rae, but found her deep in conversation with two children. Their mother, standing nearby, was listening. With no option but to try again, this time I found someone who wanted to discuss spiritual issues, and by the time we left Rae, and I could hardly wait to come again. It was literally obeying what Jesus had told me to do when he first called me:

Now something else happened that was to have far-reaching consequences in my life. Judy and Greg Blaxland, former missionaries of SAMS (South American Missionary Society) who had been in Moore College and Deac House with me, had returned to Australia for their children's schooling. Their "impossible dream," said Greg, had been to return to Venezuela after their children had grown up, and now that dream was about to be fulfilled. (I wondered whether *my* impossible dream would ever be fulfilled) Two weeks later, at 2 o'clock in the morning, I opened my eyes, feeling wide awake and alert. There was something I hadn't done, a promise I had not kept – to pray for my friends, Judy and Greg! I hadn't even found time to read their magazine. I decided to get up and pray through the SAMS magazine until I finished it.

First a cup of coffee, for it was a cold night. As I sat sipping the coffee, my ears became aware of an insistent sound in the distance. Somewhere a horse was neighing repeatedly. A horse had got out of the adjoining college grounds two weeks previously and had been hit by a car and had to be destroyed. Had a horse got out again? I'd be unable to concentrate on prayer until I investigated. One of the staff owned a horse, and perhaps it was the one in distress. Pulling on a warm coat, I quietly let myself out and went down in the lift. The nurses on duty for the hostel were surprised to see me but agreed it was best to investigate. They unlocked the front door.

Outside, the air was crisp and frosty, and as I walked I looked up at the stars, brilliant in the dark heavens. It reminded me of how I used to walk up to the hospital at night in Tanzania, and see these same stars looking down. I thought, *I wonder if Jesus might be saying to me, 'If you can come out here at two o'clock in the morning looking for a lost horse, can't you go out and look for my lost sheep?'"*

The further I walked, the further away the sound seemed to become, and when I reached our paddock, there was our staff member's horse quietly looking over the fence at me. I stroked his nose and apologised for not bringing him a piece of bread, and then, as the sound of neighing now seemed to be further away than ever, I turned round and walked back. Once more seated in my warm room I asked God to speak to me from his word before beginning my prayer vigil, and opened my Living Bible copy of *Daily Light* that I'd left lying on the table the day before. The heading of the page said: *"I am a lost sheep. Come and find me."*

By the time I'd read and prayed my way through every article in the magazine, the dawn was breaking. There was something printed on the inside of the back cover, and I thought, Since I've prayed for all the rest, I must pray about this too. Then I'll be finished. I read the writing on the cover. It said,

"Is God calling you to go as one of his missionaries to take the gospel of salvation to those who are lost? Ask him now."

I don't think God is calling me, I said honestly. But since I promised I'd pray for everything in this magazine, I'll do what it says. Kneeling down, I asked God, "Lord, do you want me to go out again as one of your missionaries?"

Ever since I'd put my trust in Jesus, I'd looked for guidance in God's word, so, now I prayerfully opened my Bible. The words that met my eyes sent a shock right through me.

"All authority in heaven and on earth has been given to me. Go therefore and make disciples of all nations, baptising them in the name of the Father and of the Son and of the Holy Spirit, teaching them to observe all that I have commanded you; And lo, I am with you always, to the close of the age." (Matthew 28:19, 20. RSV)

Could it really be, that God was calling me to go out again as an overseas missionary? But I'm established at home now, I thought. Yet how could I ignore this? God had spoken to me from his word on other occasions and I'd obeyed, so how could I disbelieve this now? Having sincerely asked in faith, I believed I must accept in faith that this was God's answer.

If so, which country was God calling me to? It couldn't be Tanzania, of that I was sure. God had closed that door. Since the magazine belonged to the South American Missionary Society, could it be that God was calling me to South America? Needing someone to counsel me, I rang Greg. There remained only one week until they left Australia, but he encouraged me to come over and have a talk.

Since I was already in my fifties, Greg said, I should test my call by trying to learn Spanish before applying to SAMS. The best way to do this, he said, would be to join a Spanish-speaking church.

On my way home I thought it all over. Greg was right – since I was not sure that my call was to South America, I should test it by trying to learn Spanish. It was still not clear which country God was calling me to, but one thing was certain. God was moving in my life again. I prayed that if the Lord was truly calling me he would confirm it so that I could be absolutely sure. Two days later the new Castle Hill Anglican Church was being opened on the border of our village. For weeks the sound of the choir practising had come floating up to me as I stood on my balcony in the evenings. Rather than attend the church's dedication on the following Saturday, I wanted to attend the first Sunday Service in the new church, and had already asked our chaplain's permission to go. So when Sunday came I was there, in the congregation.

The minister, a guest speaker, said that he had intended to speak on church unity, but at the last minute God had led him to speak on a different subject.

"All authority in heaven and on earth has been given to me. Go therefore and make disciples of all nations, baptising them in the name of the Father and of the Son and of the Holy Spirit, teaching them to observe all that I have commanded you; And lo, I am with you always, to the close of the age." Matthew 28:19, 20. RSV

"Today Jesus is speaking to you, here in this church," he said.   "He is saying to you,

Go, with my authority.

Go, with my power.

Go, with my program.

Go, with my presence."

Every word of the sermon, which was based on these four concepts, confirmed to me my call. But there was more to come. At 6am Arthur Deane spoke on God's word to Abraham. *"Look toward heaven, and number the stars, if you are able to number them........So shall your descendants be." Genesis 15:5 RSV* God took Abram outside at night to look up at the stars," Arthur Deane said, "and out there he spoke to him."

God took me outside to look up at the stars, too, I thought. I think now it may have been God who put that thought about looking for Jesus' lost sheep into my mind!

Two days later a missionary speaker came to the village, and the elderly residents expected him to tell them about his work so that they could pray for him. Instead, he gave a Bible study on the great commission, in Matthew 28:18-20.

It was the third time God had spoken to me about Jesus' great commission that same week. I remembered how the apostle Peter, after three times denying that he knew Jesus, had three times been re-commissioned by Jesus. (See John 21:15 - 17)

Could this be Jesus re-commissioning me three times over, as he did Peter? I believed that it was.

My first step of faith was to tell my mother. She had been partially paralysed by a stroke, and was being cared for in the nursing home of our Village. "I think that God is calling me to go out as a missionary again," I told her when I went to visit her.

Her reaction was immediate. "I don't know how you could even think of going away and leaving me again! God sent you home to be with me, now." But a few days later as I entered her room, she said, "Darling, there are some words going round and round in my head all the time, and I want to tell you about them."

"Yes, what are they?" I asked, coming close. Taking a deep breath, she quoted: *He who loves son or daughter more than me is not worthy of me* and *"Go into all the world and preach the Gospel!"*

Matthew 10:37 and Mark 16:15 RSV

I put my arms around her, and we laughed together with relief that God had brought us to complete agreement. Our custom was for me to read to her from "Daily Light." Asking God to speak to us, I opened the book. The heading on the page said:

I will give them one heart, and one way, that they may fear me for ever, for the good of them, and of their children after them. Jeremiah 32:39 AV

God had indeed given us one heart and mind on the matter, and my mother was back again on the same old terms with her Lord as she had always been. She had given me to God in my childhood, and she had always declared that what she had given she would never take back.

From that moment on, God blessed her. She had been unhappy in that nursing home, but soon after she was moved to another nursing home where she was much more content. Her beloved sister, Marj, moved into the village, and it was Marj's delight to spend every afternoon reading to her from her favourite devotional books. It blessed them both. Every weekend I drove them to my sister's home, and this became the highlight of the week for us all. My mother was learning, as I was, that when we give God his rightful place in our lives, he will pour out his blessing on us.

Chapter 26

I woke early on Monday morning and lay in bed, thinking. Was this the day I would take a pen and cut my links with my present life? Write my resignation, severing myself from my happy life in the Village? When I first came to the Village I had tried to learn New Testament Greek, but with my chaplaincy work it had proved too much. So now I knew that to try to learn Spanish, I must leave my work of assistant chaplain.

How could I bear to give up my lovely flat, with its purple wall-to-wall carpet and its beautiful view? I struggled to think of a way to compromise, to combine the two. Perhaps, I rationalised, I might be allowed to stay in the flat and work part-time, and study Spanish part-time.

As I lay there thinking, my clock-radio came on with the voice of the Rev Arthur Deane. It was 6am. Arthur spoke that day on Jesus' conversation with the rich young ruler who wanted to enter God's kingdom, but Jesus made one stipulation, something the young man had to do first: *"Sell all that you have and distribute to the poor, and you will have treasure in heaven; and come, follow me." Luke 18:22* RSV

The man went away, sad. He had genuinely wanted to follow Jesus, but how could he give up his riches? Did I have any riches to which I was clinging, I wondered? I didn't think so.

"You rich men and women had better go and take a good look at your gardens," Arthur Deane advised. "They wither and die, like all the riches of this world. The only riches that last forever are those of God's kingdom."

Switching off the radio, I got up and went into the lounge room. Sunlight splashed across the purple carpet. After sliding back the glass doors, I stepped out onto the balcony. My eye fell upon the pot plant that was my only garden - a fern that had belonged to my mother before a stroke had caused her to be transferred to the nursing home. I stared at it in alarm. Had I forgotten to water it? What had been fronds of lacy green was now a withered brown stump. The words of Arthur Deane echoed in my mind: "You rich people had better go and take a good look at your gardens!"

The Word of God pierced my heart and my spiritual eyes were opened. I saw that the riches I was finding it so hard to give up were my flat with its purple carpet and beautiful view, my secure job and salary, and the settled way of life that I'd now grown used to. In that instant I knew that all I was clinging to was transient, here today and gone tomorrow, like the fern. One thing only would last forever ..... the kingdom of God, and Jesus' call to go and proclaim it. I went inside and wrote my resignation.

"Where will I go?" I wondered as I ate breakfast. The memory of *Gilead,* a Christian community where I'd spent a holiday, came to me. It was the home of an Anglican deaconess named Pat Nelson. I rang her. "I believe God is calling me back to missionary service again, " I told her. "Can I come and stay at Gilead until I know what God wants me to do?"

"Of course you can!" she replied. "And if you're willing to share the cooking and housework you won't have to pay as much board." It was 8am as I hung up the telephone, and my heart was overflowing with gratitude. Within two hours of my obeying God he had provided me with a place to live, in company with others of like mind.

The name *Gilead* meant "a place of refuge." There were four of us, apart from guests, and Pat's three cats. Mushroom, the male cat, ruled the roost with a loud miow. I was glad to be learning to cook at last! Meal-times were full of fun and laughter, and if we disagreed, Pat told us that the one opposing us was "Sister Sandpaper," doing us a service by rubbing off our rough edges.

Twice a day we took turns at leading devotions, and Johanna played the organ. Don, our Chaplain, came once a month to give us Holy Communion. There was time for reflection and meditation on the word of God, and as I read the second chapter of Philippians and saw the beauty of Jesus Christ's character, I saw how seriously God views disunity amongst Christians.

Before leaving the village a resident had given me the name of a Spanish-speaking friend living near us. I visited her, and she needed someone to sit with her mother, Bita, while she went to work. "Bita" meant "grandmother." But even though I attended night classes in Spanish for a over a year and a Spanish-speaking church, and learnt to read to Bita in Spanish, by the time my work with her ended I knew I had not been called to South America. To converse in Spanish had proved too difficult for me.

If not to South America, then where? In a the youth magazine of a Spanish Baptist Church I read: *"You can run to the end of the highway but you can't run away from God."* I couldn't get the words out of my head. Was I running away from God? How could I be, when I wanted with all my heart to go wherever God wanted me to?

One morning some familiar words in the Bible caught my attention, and it was as if I were seeing them for the first time. *"Then the word of the Lord came to Jonah the second time, saying, "Arise, go to Nineveh, that great city, and proclaim to it the message that I give you." Jonah 3:1-2 RSV.*

Suddenly I saw it. Jonah had been running away from God, but God had given him a second chance. God's call to him was not to some new location, but to the same place as his first call, to Nineveh! And if God's second call to Jonah was to the same place as his first, then my second call from God could be to the same place as my first. To Africa! I'd been trying to run away to South America, thinking that God would never take me back to Africa because I'd failed him there. But now the weight of my sorrow lifted at last as I believed that God would one day take me back to Africa.

Patiently I waited for it to happen. "Failure is not final. God will open new doors of service for his forgiven child," said a charismatic priest on a cassette that I was given at that time.

But time continued creeping on, and I realised with a shock that three years had passed since God brought me to Gilead, seven since he had brought me home from Tanzania.

Why don't you forget about Africa and just settle down here at home? came a subtle whisper to my mind as I was driving one day. Pulling over, I stopped the car. "I'll ask the Lord once more about it," I said to myself. Opening the glove box I took out my New Testament, praying that God would speak to me. What I read settled the matter once and for all.

"After this many of his disciples drew back and no longer went about with him. Jesus said to the twelve, "Do you also wish to go away? Simon Peter answered him, "Lord, to whom shall we go? You have the words of eternal life." John 6:66-68 RSV

"No, Lord," I promised, "I won't go away. I believe you've

called me again, and that in your time you'll take me back to Africa. "

Very gradually, I came to the conclusion that God would not take me overseas again while my mother was still living. Although she was willing to let me go, she was now ninety-one, and it became more and more clear that because of her frailty God would not take me from her again. In the meantime I continued with the work that God had give me to do for him at home, which included the street-evangelism with Rae. When Rae could no longer go with me to Parramatta, my friend Viya took her place. We drove to Cabramatta and offered Scripture leaflets to people of varying nationalities in their own languages. The majority accepted them gladly.

My fifty-ninth birthday had gone, and my mother was nearing her ninety-second birthday. Christmas, 1987 was only a few weeks away. As I drove up Epping Road, out the side window I kept glancing at a very beautiful rainbow overhead. Rainbows always spoke to me of God's mercy.

On arrival at the nursing-home I was met by the sister, who told me, "Your mother's condition has changed." She had suffered a series of mini-strokes, but as I walked in she was still conscious. We laughed with relief that she could still talk to me, and then we cried together as I held her, for we both knew that the end might be drawing near. As each day passed, my sister and I watched her physical condition sink lower. A week later, to save her from falling out of bed; the nurses placed iron guard-rails around her bed. My mother mistook these for a fence. Ever since her stroke she had lost her old, commanding manner, and had talked in a small, child-like voice, but on her last day of consciousness, as she looked up and recognised me, her voice rang out with all its former vigour in a sharp command. *"Open it, Jo! Open the gate!"*

Those were her last words. She wanted the gate opened, but to me her words seemed to have a deeper significance. She sank into a coma, and my sister and I came and went, knowing that the end was drawing near, but not knowing just when she'd be taken from us. Thus it was that my sister had gone home, when, as I sat beside her bed watching, her face suddenly changed and I knew that God was carrying her away.

I rang to tell my sister that she had gone. My Bible reading next morning contained this promise from God:

'Your eyes will see the king in his beauty; they will behold a land that stretches afar.'   Isaiah 33:17-18 RSV

Chapter 27

Two weeks after my mother died, Pat suddenly announced that in two months' time, when she turned sixty, she was going to sell *Gilead* and move to Newcastle.

The news shook me. Where would I go? I realised that I would be turning sixty too, six months after Pat. Where would I live? I tried not to worry, but the uncertainty made me anxious. I went to visit my friend Jo Douglass in the Village. She was as warmly welcoming as ever, and we prayed about it. As I helped her to wipe the lunch dishes the text on her kitchen shelf caught my eye:

Trust in the Lord with all your heart, and do not rely on your own insight. In all your ways acknowledge him, and he will make straight your paths. Proverbs 3:5-6 RSV

The words spoke to my heart, and peace returned. God would be my guide.

Gilead was put on the market, and even before it was advertised it was sold to one of the mainline churches. They would use it in much the same way as Pat had done. Impulsively, I asked the buyers if I might stay on and work for them. They were pleased, but could not confirm it until after the sale went through. That had to wait until Pat got vacant possession of the house she'd found in Newcastle. All the guests left, and I stayed on to keep Pat company.

"I'm driving down to Stanwell Tops on Saturday for the Christian Women's Convention," an acquaintance said. "Would you like to come?" I accepted the invitation. The speaker was to be Ruth Myors. We knew each other from

RPA nursing days, and had not seen each other since. However, it was not Ruth herself, but the message she would give that would mark the day forever in my memory.

She spoke on the Israelites about to enter the promised land after forty years in the wilderness. Moses was busy organising them under Joshua's leadership, but three of the twelve tribes had already settled down on the east side of the Jordan river. Why bother to cross over and fight, when they had already received their inheritance? Moses grew angry with them.

"Shall your brethren go to war while you sit here?" he asked. *Numbers* 32:6 RSV

Ruth dramatised the scene. "You *shall not stay in Gilead!"* she shouted. *"You shall cross over with your brethren, and fight!"*

The name of the land on which the Hebrews had settled was *Gilead.*

All the way home, the words rang in my ears. *"You shall not stay in Gilead! You shall cross over with your brethren, and fight!"*

I decided not to stay on at Gilead! But I didn't take any notice of the rest of the message. Instead of getting ready to cross over, I found another way to settle down on this side of the Jordan. Why not use the money I'd inherited from my family to buy a unit in the Retirement Village? It would be somewhere to live, a base from which to go out to continue my tract ministry on the streets of Cabramatta. My aunt would be so happy to have me come to live near her, and some time in the future, when I went back to Africa, I'd have a place to come home to.

I went to see the administrative secretary of the Retirement Village. "I believe that some time in the future

I'll be going back to Africa," I told her, "and I've heard that if a resident goes overseas for longer than six months they can give up their unit and get one to replace it when they return. Is this true?"

She assured me that it was, and as I'd had my name down for some time and a suitable apartment was available, I took it. My family and friends had just the right pieces of furniture, and suddenly there it was, a beautiful little home, all ready to move into. I stood in the doorway admiring it, but as I did so some words came very softly into my mind.

"Don't love it too much. You'll be leaving it soon to go back to Africa, you know."

I made a mental note not to love the flat too much. Although it was now ready, I stayed on with Pat until she could move into her house. One afternoon at Gilead the telephone rang, and a representative of the Bible Society asked to speak to me. He was to going to preach at a church in Cabramatta, he said, and knowing of my tract ministry there he wondered whether I'd like to go with him and tell the congregation about it. I wrote down the date in my diary, but promptly forgot, and thought it was the following Sunday.

"We weren't expecting you until *next* Sunday!" the ladies of the Cabramatta church exclaimed as I walked in, "but do stay for the service. We have a missionary from Liberia to speak to us. Her name is Joy Crombie, and she's with SIM."

I didn't know where Liberia was, but I was glad my mistake had brought me to hear a missionary tell about her work. Joy was in her sixties, with blue eyes and white hair and a sparkling personality. Her name suited her, for she radiated joy. She had served as a community health nurse, first in Ethiopia and now in Liberia. She was on her way back for another term of service.

As I watched Joy's pictures of vaccination safaris in the rural villages of West Africa I remembered the mobile clinics in Tanzania. This was the kind of work I'd loved the best, and it was what I'd prayed to do. If I'd had someone like Joy to work with, I thought, perhaps I'd still be there! After she finished speaking, the people crowded around her to ask questions, and I felt I'd like to become one of her prayer-partners. "Do you have any prayer-letters with you?" I asked.

"There's just one left," she replied, handing it to me. "You're welcome to it."

Not wanting to take her last one, I found a quiet corner and sat down to read and then return it. At the end there was a list of prayer requests, and the second last one said: "Please pray for a nurse to relieve my partner-nurse for twelve months, while she goes home to Australia on leave."

Suddenly alarm bells started ringing all through me. This was what I'd been waiting for! Here was a job I could manage, one I was familiar with – my favourite kind of work. Even though I'd be turning sixty in a few months, I felt confident I could do it. Returning the letter, I said to Joy, "I might be able to come out and relieve your partner nurse, but I must go home and pray about it. When can I see you again?"

"I'm flying to a country town today," Joy said, "and I'll be returning by plane on Saturday morning. But my plane gets in just half an hour before the flight to Singapore takes off. I'll just have time to jump into a taxi and race across to the overseas terminal to check in and then board the flight."

"Even if you only have two minutes to talk, I'll see you at the overseas terminal on Saturday morning," I promised.

Setting out on the drive home, outwardly I kept calm, but inwardly I was wild with excitement. *I'm on my way to Africa! I'm on my way to Africa!* my heart sang. At the Great Western Highway the traffic lights were red, and I waited, engine idling, ready to take off the instant they changed. As soon as the lights turned green, I shot forward and turned right, in my excitement forgetting to wait for the green arrow! As I sped in front of the oncoming traffic I realised my mistake, but it was too late to stop. In the rear vision mirror I saw a line of cars crossing the highway behind me. They're probably saying *Crazy teenager!* I thought. *Calm down, Jo, or you'll have a collision!*

After calming down, I remembered my Aunt Marj, now ninety-one years of age, and looking forward to my coming into the village to be near her. How disappointed she would be if I told her I was going back to Africa. All my life she'd been so good to me. How could I leave her now, only a few months after the loss of her beloved sister, my mother? How ungrateful I'd seem to her, for she'd been like a second mother to me. The car I was driving, like every other car I'd possessed, was her gift to me, as was the money for the apartment I'd just bought.

"Dear Lord, please show me what I should do," I prayed.

And there, when I got home, was the guidance I asked for, in a verse of Scripture. *By faith Moses, when he was grown up, refused to be called the son of Pharaoh's daughter, choosing rather to share ill-treatment with the people of God. Hebrews 11:24,25 RSV (abbrev.)*

I saw that Moses may have been tempted to put the woman who had been like a mother to him before the call of God, but he resisted the temptation. Although my aunt had been so kind to me, I realised now that my duty towards her was not the same as that towards my mother. The Lord had given me seven and a half years with my mother before she died, and now, if God opened the door for me to return to his work in Africa, I must go, and ask my aunt to understand. She'd still have my sister Marjie and her husband Bill, and I knew that they would faithfully look after her.

On Saturday morning the indicator at Mascot airport announced that the Singapore flight had been delayed by ten hours. Joy didn't come, and I assumed that she'd done what I'd forgotten to do – ring the airport to confirm the flight. I decided to take my Aunt to my sister's home for lunch as planned, then return in the evening to the airport.

At 6pm I found Joy curled up on an airport lounge, reading a book. We went to dinner in the restaurant, and we marvelled that God had given us not two minutes, but two hours to get acquainted. She was from New Zealand, and had been nursing in Africa for over forty years. The *Church of God* at Cabramatta was the home church of her partner-nurse, Pauline Chilver, and Joy's only speaking engagement in Sydney was the one I had attended.

"You don't think I'm too old to come, do you?" I asked. "I'll be sixty this year."

"I'm sixty-three!" Joy laughed.

"And my back hurts if I stand too long."

"My varicose veins ache if I stand too long," she responded.

I may as well tell her all my limitations, I thought, and added, "I'm a diet-dependent diabetic, and I get low blood sugar in the mornings. I can't even think until after breakfast!"

"I get too tired to even talk in the afternoons," said Joy, "so when we go on safari, I'll drive in the mornings, and you can drive in the afternoons!"

What a relief! There would be no need to pretend. I was no chicken, but neither was Joy!

"In Liberian culture," she said, "when you get white hair like yours and mine, the people respect you more, and they call you *Old Ma*. They'll also give you a Liberian name. Mine is Ma Teni."

Joy's final instructions were to apply as soon as possible to the SIM office, so that I could come out in time to get used to the work before Pauline left. "If you don't come to Liberia," she said, "SIM won't let me stay in the village by myself. I'd dearly love to continue the work, so it's a matter of urgency. As far as I know there haven't been any other applications, and time is running out!"

We prayed together, and then it was time for her to go through the barrier.

Driving home, my heart was full of gratitude to God. I'd gone to Pauline's church on the wrong day by mistake, but it had not been the wrong day on God's calendar. My mistake had been God's appointment!

The first thing I did was to go to the SIM office and apply.

*Jo, December 1980, on day of ordination as a deaconess,
together with Deaconess Mary Andrews, Principal (left)
and Deaconess Pat Nelson of "Gilead", 1984 (right)*

Chapter 28

"Don't worry about me," my beloved Aunt Marj, now ninety-two years of age, bravely reassured me when I telephoned her from England. "You do what you have to do. I'm all right." I could scarcely speak through my tears. Unknown to us, these were the last words she would say to me, for she would die while I was in Liberia.

Liberia was the only nation of black Africa not to have been colonised, and had received a strong Christian influence through the freed slaves who returned from America. But the country was still under the influence of tribalism, fear and witchcraft, with all their ignorance and cruelty. Men's and women's secret bush societies still held sway, and boys and girls at puberty were taken into bush camps where they were indoctrinated into animistic religion and culture. In the old days some of them never returned. Human sacrifice was still known to go on, with media reports from time to time of men's bodies found in the bush with heart and sexual organs missing. In some of the provinces fighting was going on between major tribal groups, but the radio always said that the fighting was "being contained" within one or two provinces.

Since 1954 SIM had been pushing back the darkness in central, north and west Africa through the voice of radio ELWA, which stood for *Eternal Love Winning Africa*. From it the gospel went out in forty tribal languages including Gbandi, the language of the province where Joy and Pauline worked, close to the border of Guinea. Since 1965 ELWA Hospital in Monrovia had been providing medical and surgical care for people of all tribes, creeds and cultures.

From the moment I landed, excitement and joy took off in me like a car at full speed. Pauline, whom I had come to relieve, was in Monrovia for a seminar, and she warned me that I would find Liberia very different to Tanzania. But nothing could dim my expectations. I was back in Africa. The Lord was restoring to me the years that the locust had eaten (*see Joel 2:25*) and I was full of joy, overflowing with thankfulness. God had answered my prayers.

We flew in a small Bible Translator's plane over hundreds of miles of green jungle and serpentine rivers until we saw a bald rock mountain with a tiny village near it that resembled a small round eye looking up at us from the jungle. "That's Taninahun." said Pauline. "The people of the village worship that mountain."

Joy was waiting under the shade of tall forest trees at the side of the grass strip. With her were village children who had come to see the plane. After the luggage had been transferred to the Toyota Land Cruiser (the vehicle provided by CHAL, the Christian Health Association of Liberia) we waved to the pilot, and the plane quickly climbed above the trees until it was only a disappearing speck in the sky.

Our house, like several in the small village, was built of mud bricks and concrete, and from the back door we looked out into green forest trees. Among them were cotton trees which, when in bloom, would look like a troupe of dancing girls in white dresses. On the wall of my room was a picture of a mountain road with the words of God's promise: *"Be strong and of good courage; be not frightened, neither be dismayed; for the Lord your God is with you wherever you go." Joshua 1:9 RSV*

The Town Chief came to visit us and gave me a Liberian name: *Ma Jenneh*. The next day fifteen young men and women descended on the town for a six weeks' health seminar. At the end of their course each would be issued with a box of medicines to care for the health of their town.

Liberian English was a little different to ordinary English. The word *oh* occurred frequently in general conversation. For example – Instead of *What will we do?* It was – *What to do oh?* – When a word ended in a consonant, the consonant was dropped. Morning was *morni,* people were *peepo*, rice was *ri*. At prayers each morning the students sang a hymn in a language I thought was Gbandi. One morning I recognised the tune of *What a Friend we have in Jesus,* and realised they had been singing in English every morning and I had not recognised it!

I also had my own problems in being understood. Joy and I took turns at doing the radio, and many of the SIM missionaries being American, over the two-way radio they couldn't understand my accent. One morning, after twice repeating a phrase without success, I imitated an exaggerated Yankee drawl, and immediately they understood! I felt so embarrassed at the success of my act that after that I left the radio to Joy.

Joy Crombie on two-way radio, Liberia 1989

As our seminar drew to a close, I wrote a humorous health play with a spiritual application, and the students translated it into Gbandi and practised it for the approaching Christian Conference in Kolahun, our nearest town. Amongst the crowd was Morris Barwor, the Gbandi programmer for ELWA Radio. He came to us with a big smile on his face. "I liked your drama *oh*!" he said warmly. "Can you make a series like that for me to air over ELWA radio?"

During the conference several people came to Christ, and I watched as many were baptised in the river. Pauline had already gone, and when it ended Joy left for a CHAL Conference in Monrovia. I stayed on in Kolahun to wait for her return. My American hostess, Kathy, lent me her typewriter, and all day I sat tapping out plays for ELWA, based on real life experiences, such as that of a young woman suffering from a painful breast abscess. Had she been to the hospital, I asked? "*Thi no hospita bisne oh*!," she replied, (this is not hospital business) meaning that the abscess was the result of a curse, put upon her by an enemy. The only way to get cured, she believed, was to pay an exorbitant fee to a *zoe* (witch doctor) to remove the curse.

Liberia appeared to be far behind Tanzania in acceptance of modern medicine, education, and in the freedom of mind which only faith in Christ can give. The girl with the breast abscess was typical of thousands oppressed by fear of witchcraft. I remembered my pleadings with God to take me back to Tanzania, but now saw that Liberia had the greater need. Tanzania had by now trained their own nurses, and Romans 8:28 spoke to me with new meaning: *We know that in everything God works for good with those who love him, who are called according to his purpose.*

A vaccination safari was due, and with Joy away I invited

Mel, our nearest neighbour, to accompany me. High up in the hills we called on the sick son of a town chief. We were given chairs to sit on in the shade, and the boy, aged about twelve, was led out to us. He was pitifully thin after months of dysentery, and my heart went out to him as he placed a hand on my knee to steady himself so that he wouldn't fall over.

The boy's mother had died, and the chief's second wife refused to stay at the hospital with him, having her own baby to care for. Without a carer, the chief said, the hospital refused to admit him. I warned him that if he wanted his son to live he must take him to hospital immediately. He was going on a business trip he replied, and would take him when he returned. Two months later he called in to tell us that while he was away his son had died.

Mel and I continued on our safari to the village where mothers were waiting for us to vaccinate their children. It was a hot, humid day, but an eight-year-old girl stood in the sunshine clasping her thin arms around her emaciated body, hugging herself in an effort to keep warm. I found that her name was Varli, and that she had suffered from fever for over a year. She was slowly wasting away. I tried hard to persuade her mother to take the child to hospital. Who would look after her rice-field while she was away, she asked?

"She's probably got TB, but her mother thinks she's under a curse." Mel and I agreed. We left, hoping that she would think over our advice. The case, like the boy's, was one more real-life story, to teach about TB and dysentery over radio ELWA.

Joy returned and divided the work between the two of us. She did the dentistry and I treated the patients who came to our door seeking medical help. In one government hospital that had no dentist Joy pulled out one hundred and ten teeth in two days, then lay down on the back seat of the Toyota to recover while I drove home. Dental care was added to the growing list of subjects for health teaching. The plays were being translated into Gbandi by a Christian sister at Kolahun hospital, and dramatised by the Kolahun Town youth group of the SIM Church. Their leader was recording them live, and then posting them off to Monrovia to Morris Barwor who aired them over the radio. Other radio announcers at ELWA began wanting them, to translate into their own languages for their own language programs.

One day a man came running to our house shouting *"Ma Jenneh - come quickly! Ma chil i dyee!"* (my child is dying) "Bring her here," I urged, knowing that we had more chance of helping the child in our own treatment room than in a dark room with people crowding around. Even before they reached our house I could hear the raucous, laboured breathing, and alerted Joy to come and help. The father carried in his nine-year-old daughter, unconscious and with brown, blood-stained froth coming from her mouth and nostrils. In vain we tried to suck out the froth with the rubber sucker used for new-born babies, but it didn't reach down far enough.

Force feeding, known as "stuffing," was widely practised, due perhaps to fear that without sufficient food or medicine a child may die. The child was laid down and held while food or drink was stuffed into its mouth, with no regard for the necessity of taking a breath. Often the nose was held also, to force the child to swallow. As a result, many children choked to death. This grandmother admitted to "stuffing" her grand-daughter with what she called "yellow fever medicine."

"We must take her to the hospital quickly," we told them. "It's not possible to help her here." Joy got out the Toyota while I filled a bottle with drinking water and locked the house. In spite of urgency, twelve kilometers an hour was the limit at which I could drive over the bad road. Joy sat in the back with the parents and child, and behind me all the way I could hear the terrible efforts the girl was making to draw breath.

Maria, a European Sister who worked at Kolahun hospital was on duty, and heard our car. She rushed a trolley out and they laid the girl upon it. We ran with her to the operating theatre, where Maria quickly turned on the electric sucker and inserted its long rubber catheter down her throat. Vacuuming deep into her airway, the sucker was able to clear the obstruction, and as air entered her lungs she drew long, deep breaths. Her dusky colour lightened as oxygen began to circulate freely in her blood again.

Maria wheeled her out to the ward and we helped to lay her on the bed. Her grandmother and father were there, waiting anxiously. They called her name and rubbed her hands, until slowly her eyes fluttered open. It was obvious that her grandma loved her dearly, and had not meant to harm her, and it was pitiful that her ignorance had caused such suffering to the child she loved.

Many such cases were brought to the hospital, Maria told us. Only the week before, a mother had been force-feeding her baby when his sister had seen that her small brother was choking. In spite of pleas for her mother to stop, the woman persisted until she saw that the baby was not breathing. She rushed him to hospital, but on arrival he was already dead.

We drove home with heavy hearts, knowing that inhalation pneumonia was sure to follow. In spite of antibiotics, three days later the girl died. Her family brought her body home for burial beside their house, according to Gbandi custom.

One constructive thing came out of the girl's tragic death. The chief ordered all the women of the village to attend a meeting, at which he requested us to teach the dangers of force-feeding. I made a model out of two polythene tubes tied together, to demonstrate the anatomy of the body's breathing passage as distinct from its swallowing passage. A murmur of comprehension spread among the women, but some of the older ones were not going to allow their custom to be destroyed so easily by new-fangled ideas.

"Ou mothe stuffe us, a we dide die!" observed one older woman.

"You were lucky, bu many di die!" replied another. So the discussion went back and forth. The chief made "stuffing" illegal from that day, and imposed a fine on any woman caught doing it, but it still continued in secret.

Jo with Varli, Liberia 1990

Two months after I'd first seen her, Varli was still at home wasting away, her mother still refusing to take her to hospital. I told Joy about her and she suggested that I ask our chief to speak to the chief of Varli's village. I did so, warning that TB if left untreated could infect others. The chiefs responded, and someone in her village was ordered to look after the mother's crops while she took her daughter to hospital. On admission, at ten years of age Varli weighed only ten kilos. She was treated for TB, and several months later her weight had progressed to fourteen kilos. She was discharged with a supply of tablets, to continue her treatment at home. Now that her mother saw her child improving she gave up her pessimistic resignation, and became filled with hope for her daughter's recovery.

From time to time Joy reminded me that if I had not come to Taninahun she could not have still been there. When news came over the two-way radio that my Aunt Marj had suffered a stroke, Joy's words reassured me that I had not

Aunty Marj

left home in vain. When the news came two weeks later that she had passed away, my tears fell, but I thanked God for her life. "Look after my darlings," our father had said to her before he died, and she had done so as long as she was able, and my sister and her husband had taken care of her to the end. Now Aunty Marj understands why I had to leave her, I thought.

Before leaving Tanzania nine years before, I'd looked up to where the sun was still shining on Mt Kilimanjaro, while the valley where I stood had already entered the shadow. I'm going into the shadow now, I'd thought, but perhaps one day the sun will shine for me again. The sun had shone again for me in Liberia, as I'd once more been able to take part in the fight against ignorance and disease, and to proclaim the good news of Jesus' salvation and eternal life. More than ever these people would need these great truths in the days ahead, for a time of terrible suffering was coming to Liberia.

More than a year had passed, for at home Pauline extended her leave. She was seeking God's will about return, for her mother too was elderly. It finally became clear that she should come back, and it was agreed by SIM that I should go to Monrovia and continue writing health plays for the final months of my two year term of service.

What would I do after that, I wondered? I didn't feel ready for a retirement village. I still yearned to return to Tanzania, but realising that only qualified tutor-sisters were needed there now, I had to think of something else to do. My friend Genevieve had been a nurse, but she'd also taught in a Bible School. Would it be possible for me to do the same, I wondered? A letter to Bishop Mhogolo in Dodoma brought a positive response. He would like me to come and teach at Kilimatinde Bible School. My heart jumped for joy, and when CMS sent an agreement form for me to sign to be "under their umbrella" again, my joy was complete. But it would be several months before we'd know whether the Tanzanian government would grant me a work permit at sixty-two years of age.

Pauline arrived back, and the time for me to leave had come. Early on the morning of my departure, village children brought me a gift of scarlet flowers. Later I would look at the photo and wonder what had happened to those beautiful children. By the time that film was developed Liberia was plunged into a blood-bath, the Taninahun chief who had given us our Liberian names was dead, and Pauline and Joy were amongst the thousands fleeing the country.

Children say goodbye with scarlet floweres, Liberia 1990

Once again we were standing on the airstrip, then I was in the plane, we were taking off, then I was looking down on the small round eye of Taninahun looking up at us from the jungle. We were flying over the bald rock mountain for the last time, then there was nothing to be seen below except miles of green jungle.

Chapter 29

I'd been at ELWA for about two weeks when the most senior member of the SIM staff called us all together to listen to an important announcement. "The rebels are on the outskirts of Monrovia," he said. "All foreign embassies have advised their nationals to leave the country immediately."

He explained that SIM had no choice but to follow the embassies' directions. Mothers and children would be flown to England in two days' time, single women two days later. Then all men would be flown out except a skeleton staff of senior missionaries, who would stay to help the Liberian staff to keep the radio on the air, and the hospital operating.

"It's all right for you missionaries. You have somewhere to go," said Victoria, one of the SIM guest-house staff. "We have nowhere to go." She had a six-year-old daughter.

Sad and apprehensive as I felt for the Liberians, I had to think about what to do when I got to England. If SIM flew me home to Australia I would not have enough money left to return to Tanzania should my visa and work permit be granted. It would be better to stay in England until I heard, but where would I stay? I didn't have enough money for expensive accommodation. Jill, a nursing friend, had left Australia six months earlier to work in England, but she had not written, and I didn't have her address. "If only I knew where Jill was, I might have been able to stay with her," I thought regretfully.

The last thing I did before leaving for the airport was

185

to go up to the administration building and look in my mailbox. There was just one letter in it, and I stared at it in amazement. It was from Jill. "If ever you come to England," she wrote, "come and stay with me." In my life of following Jesus, God had once again shown me the next step.

SIM billeted me initially with the parents of one of their missionaries serving in Bangladesh. My thoughts were still largely focussed on what was happening to the people we'd left behind. The ELWA staff, our African friends – where were they now? Had they escaped? Hundreds of Liberians were being killed. Two WEC missionaries who didn't heed the warning to get out immediately were killed. They had served the people of Liberia for over fifty years. Pauline and Joy escaped with others, leaving everything behind.

After that it was as though a blind had been pulled down over all the places where we'd worked. There was no news except what came through the media, with stories of horrific killings. Six hundred women and children sheltering in one of the mainline churches in Monrovia appealed to the USA for help, and were all massacred by order of President Doe, who was said to have watched the killings. Thousands who were unable to escape lost their lives. Half the population fled into neighbouring countries, and disease and starvation rapidly attacked those who remained.

The SIM compound became a haven for seventeen thousand refugees, but some weeks later when word spread that the remaining missionaries were to be escorted out of the country by Charles Taylor's rebel soldiers, all the refugees fled. The rebels took over ELWA radio, and in the fighting it was burnt to the ground. The hospital likewise was severely damaged.

Were all our efforts for nothing? I read a promise in my Bible that renewed my hope:

"Therefore, my beloved brethren, be steadfast, immovable, always abounding in the work of the Lord, knowing that in the Lord, your labour is not in vain." 1 Cor. 15:58 RSV

A few days after my arrival I rang Jill. "I'm not really surprised to hear from you." she exclaimed. "I watched mothers and children from Liberia coming off the plane at Gatwick, on TV. She went on to explain her situation. "I'm nursing an elderly lady in Hemel Hempstead. You're welcome to come and stay for a week, but that's the limit I'm allowed to have visitors."

I dropped a letter in the mail to Joyce Firth with whom I'd worked at Kilimatinde. She lived at Falmouth and we had continued to correspond at times. Thanking my host and hostess for their kind hospitality, I left and took a train to Hemel Hempstead. Jill met me at the gate and we walked through a garden fragrant with spring flowers and climbed the stairs to meet her white haired patient, who was propped up against pillows in bed.

"Why not join the team?" Jill suggested to me later. "We need another night nurse. Then you could stay here as long as you're looking after Isobel." We walked down to the nursing club, and when we returned I was signed up to commence duty that same night. Jill and I celebrated on bacon and eggs followed by strawberries and cream! But when I rang SIM, the representative remarked, "I think if you look at your visitor's visa you'll find it's stamped that you're not allowed to work while you're in England."

I couldn't believe it until I took out my passport and looked, and sure enough there it was, stamped by Immigration: *"Leave to enter for six months; employment prohibited; 2 May 1990; Gatwick."*

"It's too late now for us to find anyone else for the weekend," the nursing club manager said when I rang to tell her. "Couldn't you just do from Friday to Sunday night?" I agreed gladly. Even three nights' work and wages were welcome.

"What made you go to Liberia?" Isobel asked me curiously as I sat with her that night. I explained to her that Jesus had called me to go, and shared with her the truth that motivated me – my love and gratitude to Jesus for dying on the cross to save me from hell. Isobel was keenly interested, and wanted to talk about it, for she didn't like to go to sleep early. On Monday morning when I said goodbye, she asked, "Where are you going to stay when you leave here?"

"I don't know." I replied truthfully.

"Oh, my dear, you must stay here until you find a place to go," she insisted. I was deeply grateful, and my stay lasted for a month, while I searched for a flat. At a nearby Baptist church prayer meeting one night I prayed for God to help me to find a room at a reasonable cost, and a woman named Elfrida introduced herself, offering a room at a suitable rent.

How would I occupy my time while I waited for the answer from the Tanzanian immigration, I wondered? I had neither the money nor the inclination for sight-seeing. I'd once drawn pictures to illustrate the life of Jesus for a deaf and dumb illiterate patient in Tanzania, and had a secret ambition to make a book of such pictures. Now was my opportunity! I decided to make one hundred pictures, beginning with the creation of the world, telling a little of the Old Testament, then going through the life of Christ. Elfrida's daughter kindly lent me her electric typewriter to copy an appropriate verse from the Bible for each picture.

Sketches of the life of Joseph, from "Every Picture tells a Story", 1990

As I sat there quietly drawing all day there was time to think. What had I done, offering to teach the Bible in a Swahili Bible School? Had my longing to return to Tanzania led me to take on something beyond my ability? I loved Tanzania and I loved the Bible, but did I know the historical background of the books of the Bible well enough to teach students? Moreover, although Swahili medical terms were familiar to me, Swahili theological terms were not. Added to that, my voice was soft and unsuited to prolonged speaking. Gradually I became more and more uneasy. How could I find a sure answer to my doubts? I asked God to show me.

Jill and I went for walks together at week-ends, and we discovered the old church of St John's, Hampshire Hill, and joined its congregation. The retired minister who took the services, Bob Smith, became our good friend. One Sunday he announced that he would be away for a couple of weeks as he was going to the Keswick Convention.

"The Keswick Convention!" I gasped, my eyes lighting up. I remembered the convention's magazine, *Keswick Week*, that had been such a blessing to me at Murgwanza in Tanzania.

"It's you who should to be going to Keswick," Bob exclaimed. "You've never been, and you'll probably never get the chance to go again! I'll ring and see if I can get you into an SIM house party." By the following day it was all arranged.

A way for me to check my ability to teach in Swahili in a Bible School now came to me. Dorothy Almond, a Church Army Sister who had taught the Bible for many years in Tanzania, had retired, and I knew that she lived near Keswick. She was sure to attend the convention. I wrote asking Dot whether she could bring with her some Swahili theological books.

On the way the coach stopped for lunch, and afterwards I went for a stroll in the garden. Another passenger was doing the same, and she told me she was from Sri Lanka. Her name was Subi, and after twenty years in England she had returned to Sri Lanka as a missionary. She had come back to England on a brief visit. "Let's sit together and have a talk on the return journey." she suggested.

Dot and I met in front of the main tent, and she lent me two theological books in Swahili. Taking them back to the guesthouse, I sat down to look through them, and my heart sank. The material in the books was such that I would have to study it myself before I could teach it, and if my visa suddenly came through there would not be time.

That night the convention speaker was Billy Strachan of Radio Bible Class Ministries. *"What is the Almighty Father putting his hand on in your life tonight?"* he asked. *"Is it deception? Deception about gifts? There's many a square peg in a round hole in Christian service. Search your heart tonight and see whether you have been deceiving yourself and others about your gifts."*

God had my full attention now. First the books, and now this! I saw that I had deceived myself and others in offering to teach in a Tanzanian Bible School.

What could I do? The contract was already signed with CMS and the African Bishop. I couldn't bring myself to tell them I'd "changed my mind!" Instead, I prayed that if God didn't want me to go he would prevent my visa from being granted.

Two nights later Billy Strachan spoke again.

"I'm only going to speak about one gift tonight," he said. "The gift of helping others is named in 1 Corinthians 12:28".

"That's my gift," I thought, "the practical gift. It's what I've been doing all these years when I've been nursing."

Billy related a true story about a minister who had been President of the Uniting Church in Australia. (I knew him. He had been in charge of the ELM Centre when I had done a course in Caring Communications there.)

As a young man he had attended a youth camp where everyone was allotted duties. His was to be the "medical officer." He was pleased by the title, and imagined himself going around wearing a white coat. His first job was to clean the toilets! And the first toilet he came to was very dirty. Someone had misfired! (the Keswick crowd roared with laughter). The young man laid down his tools of office and walked away. Later he was mortified to hear that the Camp Commandant had cleaned up the mess.

When that young man became a leader and later a minister, it was noted of him that at any camp he led he always put his own name down to clean the toilets!

As soon as Billy mentioned toilets, I knew that God was speaking to me. Toilets, throughout my nursing career, had been my "specialty." Memorable toilets in my life had been those I had to make spotless as a junior nurse, toilets whose cleaning I had to supervise in the mental hospital, toilets in the children's ward at Mvumi hospital that I was instructed to get "cleaned up," and toilets I encouraged leprosy patients to clean at Hombolo. I remembered them all.

I don't know what God wants me to do next, I thought as I followed the crowd out of the big tent, but I wouldn't be surprised if it might involve toilets again somewhere!

Chapter 30

"If you don't get a visa for Tanzania, come to Sri Lanka," Subi suggested. We were travelling back to London on the bus together as arranged, and I had confided my dilemma to her.

Sri Lanka! It had never entered my head before. "I really only want to work in Africa," I said frankly.

"Promise me that if you don't get your visa for Tanzania you'll think about coming to Sri Lanka." she insisted. "I need a nurse to help me start a creche in a poor area."

"I'll think about it and let you know," was all I could promise, and we exchanged addresses. On arrival back I found that Elfrida's student boarder was returning, and would need the room. I wrote again to Joyce Firth, and received a letter in reply. She'd been sick the first time I'd asked her, but now she was better. She said she felt it was God's will for me to stay with her for the rest of my time in England. My prayers had been answered!

It was twenty-five years since Joyce and I had parted at Kilimatinde, yet it seemed only yesterday as we caught up on each other's news and reminisced about old times. Every day I worked on my picture gospel, and every evening we took Trixie, her King Charles Spaniel, for a walk around picturesque Falmouth town or along the sea front.

At last the long-awaited letter arrived from Tanzania. At sixty-two I was considered too old to receive a work permit, and the visa had been refused. With a sigh of relief I thanked God. But now I had to make a decision regarding Sri Lanka!

I didn't want to go there, but Subi was so sure it was God's will that I found it difficult to resist her insistence. When uncertain about anything important I knew that whatever I decided, as soon as my decision was made, I 'd feel the opposite might be right.

I booked for Colombo.

But if Tanzania had refused a visa because of my age, wouldn't Sri Lanka do the same? Wasn't I wasting my money flying there when it would cost a lot less to go straight home? I went to the airways office and changed my booking to Sydney. Then I wrote to Subi, who had already left for Colombo.

She sent a telegram saying I should come, and that her friend Brother Sam would help me to get a visa. Once more I changed my ticket back to Colombo. But as soon as I'd done so, doubts again assailed me. Who was Brother Sam? How could he help to get me a visa? How did I know I could trust him? And even if he thought he could help, wouldn't it be better for me to go home and wait? If he got me a visa I could go to Colombo. I wrote to Subi again, and went to the airways office and changed my booking back to Sydney.

There was less than one week now before my British visa would expire, and I was sure I couldn't change my mind again. Joyce invited a friend to an evening meal, and after dinner we sat in the lounge room talking, over coffee. As her habit sometimes was, Joyce fell asleep in her chair. This left me to entertain the visitor, and I didn't know what to talk about. In an effort to interest her, I brought out my photographs of Liberia, and we looked at them together.

"And this one is of where we turned back," I commented, holding a photograph of a man digging in a sea of mud while our Toyota Land Cruiser stood in the background.

My words rang a note of warning in my head. It all came back to me – how the man had threatened "to deal with me" when he'd finished digging because I'd taken his photo without his permission, and how I'd been afraid of his threat and had persuaded Joy to turn back. As a result, we'd had another call that night and had got stuck in the mud after all. I'd vowed never to turn back again. Was I turning back now, from Sri Lanka?

Joyce woke up from her nap and got the supper, and after the guest had gone I went upstairs to my room and knelt down. "Lord, am I turning back from Sri Lanka?" I asked God. As I opened my Bible, the words that met my eyes shocked me!

"No one who puts his hand to the plough and looks back is fit for the kingdom of God. Luke 9:62 RSV

For the first time I'd been given a direct word from the Lord. I knew now that it was not just Subi, but Jesus, calling me to Sri Lanka. What God had for me to do there I had no idea, but now I believed that, like Tanzania and Liberia, this was a call from the Lord, and now that I knew it was from Jesus, I wouldn't turn back.

"Whatever will Joyce and the airways office girl say!" I groaned. But Joyce was undismayed. She had understood my uncertainty – that I couldn't go unless I was sure it was from God. Assurance now attached wings to my feet as early the next morning I flew down the hill to the airways office. The girl was very helpful, and found a booking for me in two days time – just one day before my English visa expired. I sent a telegram to Subi saying, "I'm coming!"

How glad both Joyce and I were that God had given

us this time together. We had experienced some differences of opinion in the past, but now we both knew that it had made no difference to our friendship. It was more firmly cemented than ever.

Several months after I'd left England, a neighbour returned a letter I'd written to Joyce. She told me that one Sunday morning before she went to church, Joyce had taken Trixie out into the garden. There in the garden, instead of going to church, Joyce had suddenly gone to heaven.

Chapter 31

After two months amongst the tea plantations and waterfalls of Sri Lanka's green hills, it gradually became clear that Subi's dream of starting a creche at Rosella could not be implemented. I didn't feel anxious about what I should do, because my decision to come had not been based on Subi's persuasion, but on the warning I'd received from the Lord Jesus not to turn back. Therefore, somewhere in Sri Lanka I believed that God had something for me to do. I believed he would show me what it was.

A friend booked a bed for me at the women's hostel of the Colombo City Mission of the Methodist church. Subi went to her brother's house and I hired a trishaw (three-wheel taxi) and directed the driver to the densely populated industrial area of Pettah. Lottery ticket sellers shouted over loudspeakers and roadside stall owners loudly advertised their wares as the trishaw wove its way through the narrow streets, and turned into the driveway of a white painted church. The security guard helped me to carry my luggage up to the second floor, where I was greeted by a stately, grey-haired woman wearing an attractive sari. She was the womens' hostel supervisor, Mrs Murray, known to the girls as Jackie Aunty, and she showed me into an airy bedroom which I would share with three other women. The large sitting room opened onto the roof, to which we could retreat to watch the sunrise, the sunset and the stars. It was a place to pray, in the midst of a busy city.

Everyone was Sri Lankan, but most of the young women knew English, and like Jackie were so welcoming I felt I'd

197

come home. They called me "Jo Aunty." On Christmas Eve, as the hands of the clock pointed to midnight, we all went out onto the roof, and the dark sky lit up with thousands of coloured stars. Bells began to ring all over Colombo, while crackers pop-popped in the dark streets below.

My visa had been extended to three months, and each day I continued to work on my book, *Every Picture Tells a Story* – one hundred pictures, with Bible verses, telling the story of Jesus' life. At last it was finished. A new friend, Prianthi, helped me to get it printed, five hundred copies in Sinhala, three hundred in Tamil and two hundred in English. The Methodist Church offered to distribute them, most to Sunday Schools and some to the deaf children's school. Some would be for children I was destined to meet on the streets. For those who couldn't read, the pictures would tell the story.

One day as I was walking along the upstairs walkway of a shopping complex near the mission, I happened to glance down into the street below. An old man was lying in a cart, and his emaciated appearance spoke of severe illness. Beside him in the cart sat a little boy of about seven, playing. I went down to them. The man knew only a little English. He simply held out his hands and pointed to his feet. The skin was cracked and oozing with severe dermatitis. Returning to the mission I brought back our youth-worker to translate for me, and offered to take the old man to the government hospital. He agreed, and his grandson came with us. His dermatitis was due to an allergy to tablets he was on for TB, and he was admitted, to commence a new treatment regime. I brought his grandson back to the street where I'd found them, and invited him to come to me every morning for breakfast while his grandfather was in hospital. He claimed to be ten, but was so small I nicknamed him "Tom Thumb."

Tom Thumb came every morning and stood in the court-yard and shouted up to me, *Sudu nona! Badigini!* "White lady! Hungry!" He liked the tea with lots of milk and sugar and the bread and margarine that I gave him, and very soon began bringing other boys. I visited them in the street where they hung out. Boys came from many places in the island to seek work in the markets, and lived together on the streets. Several lived at the bus station, and two whom I judged to be about eleven years old showed me the pieces of cardboard torn from cartons on which they slept. If they failed to find work they searched the refuse bins outside shops for unfinished food packets.

In the course of their rough work, boys often injured themselves, and without proper treatment their injuries became infected. One boy was suffering from conjunctivitis and had bought a tube of eye ointment, and another boy was putting it in his eyes for him. The boy's work was riding the trains with an elderly blind beggar, helping him on and off at stations. I bought a supply of eye ointment, medicines and dressings, and told the boys to come to me at the mission for treatment. Children from the mission's creche and primary school also began coming, and the courtyard became our regular treatment place.

Jackie was a champion of all the disadvantaged children in the area, and one afternoon she took me to meet the principal of the mission's school. They had formerly had a clinic he said, until seven years previously when racial rioting had caused their building to be burnt down. It had since been re-built, and if they had a nurse they could start a clinic again. I went to see the superintendent, and he confirmed that if I were willing to stay and work with them, the Methodist Church would give me a missionary visa, and they would renovate another building and open a clinic there. I gave him my references, but knew I had to be sure about whether this was the work for which God had brought me to Sri Lanka. I asked God to show me.

Soon after, I found a sick boy lying on the ground in a dark corner of the shopping complex. I took him to the outpatients department of the general hospital, and the number he was given was 480. Did we have to wait for 479 patients ahead of us to be seen? No wonder they wanted clinics in addition to the hospital, I thought! But perhaps, I thought hopefully, the first ticket that day might be 400! I never found out, for a distant thud caused all the patients to jump up and run out of the building. We followed, running along the street with the crowd to where police were already cordoning off an area. Ambulances, taxis and three-wheelers began to tear past carrying dead and injured people. The thud had been a terrorist bomb blast.

It was hard to realise that at the exact moment we heard the detonation, lives had been terminated, and others had been maimed for life. Some, having lost limbs, would have to sit on the roadside and beg, like the young man who sat on the footpath where I passed on my way to the bus. He had lost both hands and one foot. Another had lost both hands and both feet and was carried from door to door on his friend's back, begging. We did not go back to the hospital that day but returned to the mission, and rang Lily, our doctor and my friend, and she called in after work.

Before starting a clinic I wanted to see one in operation, so I went to see an all Sri Lankan one at an Anglican Church. After a brief look, I turned to go, but the sister in charge insisted I go in and meet the doctor. He asked me who I was and where I came from, and I told him a little about myself.

Then came a barrage of questions. "Why did you leave Liberia? You've got an Irish name. Did you visit your Irish relatives while you were in England? Why did you come to

Sri Lanka? If you're an Anglican, why do you want to work at a mission of another denomination? If you were a real missionary," he finished accusingly, "you would go to your Bishop and offer to work wherever he places you!"

I escaped as quickly as I could, and outside gave way to tears of shock at being accused of possibly being a spy! It seemed obvious to me that any foreigner wishing to work in the island could be suspect, and in an effort to allay suspicion I decided to follow the doctor's advice and investigate missions of my own church. I made an appointment to see the Anglican Bishop.

On the morning of my appointment I set out early, walking briskly down the road. Passing the street in which the boys lived, I glanced along it. Tom Thumb saw me and ran towards me, waving his arms and shouting, "Jo Aunty! Jo Aunty!" He led me to a boy whose arm was hanging from the elbow in an unnatural manner. He was a poor, intellectually disabled boy and very fearful, but he agreed to come with me in a taxi to the hospital. Tom Thumb came too, and I called at the mission and went to my room to get some money. When I came out the boy had gone. He had run away.

I went inside and made a phonecall, cancelling my appointment with the bishop. The boy with the broken arm had convinced me that the boys needed someone to care for them, and that they were the reason why God had brought me to Sri Lanka.

The superintendent's term of office had finished, and a new superintendent, the Rev Harold Fernando, would be my boss. What would I call him? Mr Fernando? Sir? Most of the staff called him "Reverend Harold," and since this seemed appropriate, I did the same. Two things may have been responsible for setting us off on a shaky footing. One was that I was a mystery to him. I'd given my references to his predecessor, but somehow he never saw them, and he didn't ask me for more. The other thing that possibly made him suspicious of me was that he knew the doctor I'd met at the Anglican Clinic. He often teased me about the doctor's suspicions! But perhaps it was as a precaution just in case the doctor was right, that the Rev Harold told me I was not to have any visitors! I had no idea that I was under surveillance.

In order to obtain a resident's visa I needed to leave the country and come back when the visa was granted. The boys accompanied me to the airport in the mission van, and it was only later as I looked at their photos which I took that day that I saw in their faces both sorrow and fear. They were afraid I might not return!

But I did return, and brought with me loving gifts from my family and my church, which at this time was Holy Trinity at Baulkham Hills. The day after I arrived back, twenty-five excited boys gathered in our courtyard.

"What are all these boys doing here?" the Rev Harold asked, startled to see so many. I explained they'd come to receive their gifts. Each boy went away wearing an Australian T-shirt and shorts, and that evening the courtyard hosted groups of boys playing with toy cars and plastic roads, wooden trains and train lines. From there on the boys came every evening, and Mrs Alexander, the wife of a staff member, began teaching them to read and write. When one of the residents complained that the courtyard's privacy had gone the Rev Harold turned a deaf ear. He was keen to start something for the street children even if it meant tolerating a stranger in their midst.

Renovation of the old building began. I continued to treat patients in the courtyard, waiting eagerly for the clinic to be opened.

Chapter 32

Susi, a twelve-year-old boy, contracted typhoid, and I took him to hospital. For two weeks he lay silently looking up at me with a shy smile when I came to visit him, being kept alive on a drip. When he was discharged he was still very weak. He came to us scarcely able to walk under the heavy load that his boss had burdened him with. He lay down in our car park, where he stayed for five days as we fed and cared for him. His boss didn't come to look for him, so our doctor's brother, Huxley, arranged light work for him in a private home. At 11pm one night six months later the boy's employer brought him back and left him at our gates. There had been a household dispute, and he was sacked. He had never received any of his promised wages. He returned to school and worked early in the morning and after school in the market to make a living.

Huxley, who had got him the job, felt bad about it. He rang Susi's boss, and I rang too, but months passed and the promised wages didn't come. One day Huxley roared into our courtyard on his motor bike and showed me a bundle of bank notes. He had gone to Susi's employer's office and demanded the boy's wages, refusing to leave until he got them. We went straight to the school, and Huxley gave the boy his money.

Two days later Dr Lily came to tell me that Huxley had been run over and killed on the street early that morning. We were all shocked and saddened, but comforted by what had taken place two days before. It seemed as if God, knowing what was going to happen, had prompted Huxley to complete his unfinished business for the Lord before leaving this world. Susi came with us to the funeral, no doubt the first Christian funeral he had ever been to.

The clinic opened at last. Next to it was a large room as yet undesigned, and I requested it for the boys. The Rev Harold agreed, and their first question was, "Can we sleep in it?"

"Not yet," I replied, "But pray and ask God, and perhaps the time might come when you can." They were also given the use of the toilets and shower block, and a verandah to hang their clothes to dry. For the first time the boys were able to take pride in keeping clean.

The boys tried to teach me Sinhala, but they didn't know how to go about it, and the background noise distracted me. I prayed that God would give me a teacher who was a woman, my own age, and preferably a trained teacher, who would come and teach me in the peace and quiet of my own room. A tall order? But not too tall for God! Soon after, I saw a sari-clad woman standing in our drive-way looking up at a notice about a mission that was to commence that afternoon. "What kind of mission will it be?" she asked politely in excellent English.

I told her, adding, "But you're too early. It doesn't commence for more than an hour yet. I'm just going to buy milk. Would you like to come with me?" She fell into step beside me, and we talked as we walked. Her name was Celia, and she was a teacher at the Bishop's College where she had taught for thirty-three years. She was exactly my own age, and soon to retire. After buying the milk I invited her up to our boys' room. For the next hour she talked to the boys and translated for me, while I went through the clothes cupboard. When the time came for her to go, I thanked her for her help, but she protested. "Don't thank me – it's a privilege! I'd like to help you regularly. I'm willing to come once a week after school if there's anything I can do."

"Well, there *is* a way you could help," I replied. "I need someone to help me to learn Sinhala."

"I'd love to help you," she exclaimed. "There's no need to pay me. I'd count it a privilege." From that day on Celia came once a week, and our friendship grew, as did my friendship with Lily, the doctor who gave her services to the clinic, and her husband Lackshman. But the language was difficult to learn. My age and the humidity were against me. I had to content myself with learning such essential phrases as *"Stop that noise, stop fighting, wash your clothes, etc"* and for the clinic, *"Put your foot up, hold still, don't touch,"* and other instructions. I taped them to the clinic wall and quoted them at appropriate times.

Margaret, an English social worker, came to help, and being young and having a flair for language she was soon able to converse in Sinhala. She loved the boys and they loved her, and we all enjoyed visits to her house. When her term of service ended we missed her greatly.

I wanted the boys to go to school, but it became increasingly clear that they were unsuitable to participate in normal school. They had never been to school before, they did not attend regularly, and they found it very difficult to be early. One day I felt so frustrated that I wished I had a punching-bag ! Since I didn't, I threw my bread-board on the floor to see if that would help. It didn't. I was angry, and was angry with myself for getting angry. *Why am I getting so angry, Lord ?* I asked.

In my Bible I read, *And the Lord said, "Do you do well to be angry?" Jonah 4:4 RSV* God showed Jonah that his greatest need was to love the people of Nineveh and to be patient with their ignorance, for they *"did not know their right hand from their left" Jonah 4:11 RSV* I saw that my need was to love the people of Sri Lanka and to be very patient with the boys.

Selwyn Hughes, author of *Every Day With Jesus*, was visiting the island, and I attended his seminars. His talk helped me to see the answer to my problem. Anger can be a result of having unrealistic goals, he said, and continual frustration of those goals leads to explosions of anger. I saw that my frustration was caused by not being able to get the boys to go school. My great desire was to see them not only cared for, but educated. All this in the few short years I'd have with them! It was indeed an unrealistic goal.

I saw now that it had to be a long-term project, and that the boys needed long-term loving care and understanding, and in the future some of them might see the desirability of an education. The person who would carry on the work after I'd gone might see this happen. I could just thank God for granting me the privilege of starting the work, and pray for a dedicated person to carry it on when the time came for me to go home.

Chapter 33

One afternoon Tom Thumb came in very excited. He'd found a new school, he said, where it didn't matter if children were late for school, or irregular in attendance! They could work in the market from 4am to 9am if they wanted to, and then go to school. There was lots of interesting hand-work, and trips to places of national fame, as well as camping. The school was part of an NGO *(Non-government organisation)* project, especially for street-dwelling families.

Like birds wheeling and flying away, the boys followed Tom Thumb, and returned each evening for showers and a meal, and for treatment of the day's wounds.

The wet season had come and heavy rains lashed down, turning the ground floor of the shopping centre into a swimming pool for the boys. They claimed the bus station was uninhabitable, and begged to be allowed to sleep under the cover of our car park. I sent up a prayer to the Lord and then asked the Rev Harold. To my delight he agreed. "It will be the first step towards a more permanent sleeping arrangement," he said, and informed me that the organisation that funded the mission's creche had just accepted a project for a night shelter for the boys. Rooms adjoining the clinic would be renovated for it.

There was much fun unrolling sleeping mats in the car park, and getting the boys settled down for the night. It became a regular game as I prowled around with my stick, threatening to hit the first boy who moved. If anyone stirred, I brought my stick down with a loud thud on the concrete floor, and the startling sound was enough to keep order. We all enjoyed the game, and when gentle, regular breathing told me all were sleeping I stole upstairs. The security man guarded them and us, and God watched over us all.

The Shelter opened at last, and with great exuberance the boys came in. There was a room for big boys and a separate one for small boys, plus one each for the cook and me. The superintendent threatened that if the boys broke the furniture he'd have the place turned into an old peoples' home!

Equipment for metal work training was donated plus exercise machines for recreation, a gift from the Australian High Commission, due to a visit from Matthew Neuhaus (ex-missionary kid of Tanzania, now grown up and employed in Australia's Dept of Foreign Affairs). The boys especially loved to jump on the trampolines!

A few weeks after the opening, a representative from the funding organisation came to see the new project in operation. There was a celebration dinner, accompanied by speeches. The boys' twelve-year-old leader made a speech which was translated into English.

"Before Jo Aunty came," he said, "when we needed a bath we went to the beach for a swim. We smelt so bad the people in the train moved away from us. But now we can keep clean, and we have somewhere safe to sleep and good food to eat. We want to thank you very much."

I loved the boys and I loved my work, but I was getting older. My ears had started ringing with tinnitus and the boys' shouting and my having to shout at them became an increasing problem to me. I prayed that God would find a suitable man to become Warden, so that I could go home. Time passed and no one had been found, so I asked the superintendent for a youth worker. Shortly afterwards a young Sri Lankan man joined the staff. I determined to teach him everything including clinic skills, so that he could take my place when I went home on leave. My friends in Newcastle, Pat and Wilsie, had invited me to come home once a year for a two-week break, and in Sydney Brian and Sue always found a bed for me.

The youth worker was God's provision. He had a passion for cleanliness. His way of dealing with the clothes cupboard was to personally re-wash all the boys' clothes. He took over much of the routine work, including shopping and taking boys to medical and dental appointments. But he was loath to discipline the boys, so this remained my job.

Little boys annoyed big boys and big boys hit little boys, and there were fights. When the boys would not come to literacy classes I took away their marbles, until my pockets bulged with marbles. If they wouldn't shower before watching TV in the evenings I stood with my finger on the control button, threatening to switch the TV off, until peer pressure forced the rebels to bathe. One little boy was so rebellious about a bath that I put him in the bathing recess and poured water over him, wetting myself in the process!

I'd been right in thinking that somewhere there might again be toilets for me to supervise. Before long, chains wouldn't pull and taps disappeared off showers. Karate kicks broke locker doors, and when five were broken I knew I had to report it to the superintendent. Would he carry out his threat and turn the place into an old peoples' home? Instead, he received the news without dismay. "We need stronger locker doors," he remarked mildly. "I'll get the carpenter to see to it."

I came to the conclusion that the Rev Harold's "bark was worse than his bite."

Chapter 34

The new year of 1995 came in with its spectacular fireworks display in the skies and the popping of crackers all round us. Boys who had been eleven and twelve when I first came were now fifteen going on sixteen. I had watched the boys grow up, and had seen new ones come in. Fifteen was the official age limit for staying in the shelter, and the boys continued to say they were fifteen when we suspected some had turned sixteen or more.

Big boys inevitably quarrelled with the security men, and I worried lest they be reported and thrown out. The lifestyle of some, after they left, made me sad and discouraged, and doubts gradually began to trouble me. What sort of men would our boys be in the twenty-first century, now so close? Would all our activities be, as some had predicted, in vain? Was what we were doing worth while?

Something that helped me to believe that it was worthwhile was that, though some boys preferred to remain on the streets, others chose to come and live in the shelter. This indicated that some boys had a desire for a different kind of lifestyle. Every boy who came in wanted a key for his own locker. It was the one place in the world where he could keep his belongings. There was one locker that always had clean, neatly folded clothes, and the boy who owned it was an encouragement to me.

But there was another locker that made me very sad. It contained the clothes and Christmas gifts of a sensitive eleven-year-old boy who was unhappy. He confided to me one day that he was being teased on his way home from school, and that he was thinking of running away. Two weeks later he disappeared. I sent boys to look for him and kept all his things in his locker, hoping that one day he might return, but he never did. Five months later his body was found on a lonely country road. Newspapers said that two brothers who had a history of depraved sex had been charged with his murder. We all mourned his tragic death.

In a CMS magazine which was sent to me, I saw that Bishop Ken Short was to lead the Bible Studies at the "Maydays" gathering in the Blue Mountains, at home. Needing fresh assurance from the Lord that I was truly in the place of his appointment, I longed to go, and what better place to seek guidance than at CMS "Maydays" I thought? My pension cheques were sufficient to cover the fare, and so I asked the Rev Harold for two weeks leave. As always, he granted it. It was the sixth time I'd been home in five years.

The studies were on God's instruction to the prophet Samuel, now an old man, to go to Bethlehem and secretly anoint one of Jesse's sons to be the next king of Israel.

"Samuel was a broken man," said the Bishop. "He was still grieving over God's rejection of Saul as king, and he was a failure as far as disciplining his own sons was concerned. But God told him, `Samuel, I will tell you how to cope with failure. I have something for you to do, today! Fill your horn with oil! There is no better thing that you are going to do in all your life than the thing that you are going to do as an old man, for you are going to set a young man on his way, for God.`"

"It was a risky thing for Samuel to do with Saul still on the throne," Bishop Short continued, "and it called for faith and courage on the part of Samuel. But faith, courage and obedience are the hallmark of all God's servants, in the long list recorded in Hebrews Chapter 11.

What did Samuel have to do? He had to fill the horn with oil, listen to the voice of God, walk to Bethlehem, and do what he was told. Any oldie can do that!"

"Then get on your way," the Lord said to Samuel. "Don't be weighed down by yesterday's failures. There is something new for you to do, today!"

Samuel obeyed.

The eldest son was a good-looking man, but God told his servant, "Don't consider his appearance or his height, for I have rejected him. The Lord does not look at things that man looks at. Man looks at the outward appearance, but the Lord looks at the heart."

As each of Jesse's sons passed before him the Spirit of God told Samuel, "The Lord has not chosen him." When the last boy had been interviewed, Samuel asked Jesse, "Have you any more sons?"

"Only the youngest" their father replied. "He's out minding the sheep."

"Bring him," Samuel ordered.

The youngest had seemed unimportant to Jesse, but he was the reason God had brought his servant Samuel to Bethlehem. The boy was David, Israel's future king, the one of whose line the Lord Jesus Christ would eventually be born. Samuel took out his vial of sacred oil and poured it upon young David's head.

"We too are sent out by God with a vial of holy oil," Ken said. "Like Samuel, we don't know which of those to whom we go will receive the divine anointing.

Fill your horn with oil, and go. Go, not knowing, but

believing."

Ken asked in conclusion, "What has the Lord been saying to you this morning?"

I felt I knew what the Lord was saying to me. Go back to the boys, not knowing, but believing that amongst them there will be one boy, and perhaps more than one, whom the Lord will anoint with his Holy Spirit, to be his, to love and to serve him forever.

I went back, glad to be with the boys again. A few months later, those in authority saw the need for a Sri Lankan man to be in charge of the boys. They chose the young man I had trained and made him Acting-Warden, until a suitable older man could be found. I was asked to carry on the work of the clinic. The new Superintendent, the Reverend Daniel Koilpillai, wanted me to consider starting a girls' ministry in the new year. But I believed God's time for me to go home had come.

Goodbye to the boys, Colombo 1995

On the twenty second of December, 1995, I flew out of Colombo for the last time.

I have written this book as a testimony to the reality of the risen, living Jesus, who communicates with all those who believe. I am not worthy, as John the Baptist said, even to untie Jesus' sandals, but imperfect as I am, I cannot help but tell about the reality of Jesus Christ in my life. He has guided me, warned me, disciplined me, has given me repentance and has forgiven my many sins. He has comforted and encouraged me, and all through his holy word, the Bible. In addition he has guided the circumstances of my life step by step, and has spoken to me on occasions directly through his Holy Spirit. I have recorded some of these occasions in order to encourage others who may encounter some of the same kind of problems in life as I did.

After he rose from the dead Jesus appeared to his disciples many times, but the first time he did so his disciple Thomas was not present. The others told Thomas, "We have seen the Lord!" But Thomas would not believe.

"Have you believed because you have seen me?" Jesus said to Thomas. "Blessed are those who have not seen, and yet believe." John 20:24-29 RSV

Epilogue

What is happening in the twenty-first century in those places where I worked and visited, and where my heart is still?

Max Collison, a medical student whom I met at Hombolo when he was doing a year's voluntary service at Berega Hospital, returned there to work after qualifying as a doctor. Hanna Steffens from Germany came to relieve Alma in looking after the orphans, and Max and Hanna married. With three children of their own, they now serve God with CMS in the slums of Nairobi, where Max is opening medical clinics that provide care for those who otherwise would have none. These are staffed largely by training volunteers from Nairobi's churches. Another CMS doctor, Joe Radkovic with his wife Sue and their two children, have joined Max and Hanna, and are working to set up maternity clinics in these slum areas where people struggle to exist.

Dr Russell Clark from Sydney is teaching medical students at Kilimanjaro Christian Medical Centre and his wife Kay teaches in the Bible School. Keren Boyd, a nurse, with Dr Steve Bradford, his wife Kate and their four children are serving with CMS at Berega Hospital. Kate also teaches at the Lay Training Centre.

The Christian Lay Training Centre at Berega and Morogoro Bible School are supported by CNEC/Partners International in Sydney, an interdenominational mission which sponsors national Christian workers in many poor countries. Like CMS and SIM, CNEC operates through the free-will offerings of God's people.

Mvumi Hospital continues its valuable work, and CMS Dr Michael Burke, his wife Jean and their three children are stationed in Dodoma, from where Michael goes out to visit twelve hospitals and thirty health centres and endeavours to establish AIDS control. Jean too has a vital and compassionate role in ministering to AIDS patients and orphans, as does Annette Gill at Murgwanza Hospital. At Kilimatinde Hospital and Bible School the good work goes on, and sisters from the German Church carry on the work that Lesley started at Kalinzi.

In Liberia, ELWA Radio and hospital have been rebuilt, and the church is struggling to get re-established after years of fighting in the country. Near the border of Guinea where we worked, fighting has again erupted, causing thousands to flee into Guinea and Sierra Leone. Morris Barwor, the Gbandi tribal announcer who aired our health and Bible plays over Radio ELWA, was captured by rebels along with his wife and six children in 2001, but with God's help managed to escape to Sierra Leone. They are amongst the 40,000 Liberians in five refugee camps there. "We came with nothing, only our lives," he wrote to Don Walker, formerly of SIM Liberia.

The street boys' hostel in Colombo continued until the year 2001 with approximately eighteen young boys under twelve, when funding failed and the boys were transferred into the Methodist Church's Boys' Industrial Home. There they continue to receive education and to learn a trade.

The European Christian Mission continues to print literature in various languages which enables many including myself to reach out to people of other nationalities, and some of the overseas students respond to an invitation to come and study the Bible in easy English, like those pictured with me in the front of this book.

Many people are asking, "Are we alone in the universe, or is there someone out there?" *There certainly is Someone out there. He is also here with us.* The Apostle Paul declared *"I heard a voice"*.... (Acts 22:7) Many people have testified to hearing the voice of the Holy Spirit of God speak to them, and I also have testified to this in my book. All those I've mentioned who are serving God in the places I've listed have heard God speak to them.

To all who are willing to listen, God speaks through his word the Bible. Jesus promised, *"My sheep hear my voice and I know them, and they follow me. (John 10:27 RSV)*